TEACHING CHILDREN
TO CLEAN

The Ready-Set-Go Solution That Works!

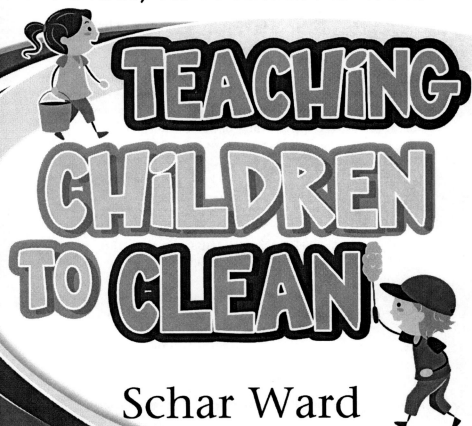

TEACHING CHILDREN TO CLEAN

Schar Ward

Teaching Children To Clean:
The Ready-Set-Go Solution That Works!

Copyright © 2016 Schar Ward

All rights reserved. No part of this book may be reproduced or transmitted in any form or by any means, electronic or mechanical, including photocopying, recording, or by any information storage and retrieval system, without written permission from the publisher.

Universal-Publishers Boca Raton, Florida · USA
2017
www.universal-publishers.com

978-1-62734-083-0 (paperback)
978-1-62734-084-7 (Epub)

Cover design by Luana Parrella
Interior layout by Viktoria Szalma

Publisher's Cataloging-in-Publication Data

Names: Ward, Schar.

Title: Teaching children to clean : the ready-set-go solution that works! / Schar Ward.

Description: Boca Raton, FL : Universal Publishers, 2017.

Identifiers: LCCN 2016955778 | ISBN 978-1-62734-083-0 (pbk.) | ISBN 978-1-62734-084-7 (EPUB ebook)

Subjects: LCSH: House cleaning--Handbooks, manuals, etc. | Housekeeping. | Orderliness. | Parents--Life skills guides. | BISAC: HOUSE & HOME / Cleaning, Caretaking & Organizing. | FAMILY & RELATIONSHIPS / Parenting / General.

Classification: LCC TX324 .W37 2017 (print) | LCC TX324 (ebook) | DDC 648/.5--dc23.

TABLE OF CONTENTS

DEDICATION

To my children, Debbie, Robert, and Betty.

I wasn't always sure I was doing things right when you were growing up, but watching you prepare a meal, set a beautiful table, plan a memorable party and maintain your homes were the inspiration for writing this book. You make me proud to say I'm your mom, and I want other parents to have the same satisfaction of watching their children become responsible, capable and considerate adults who are in charge of their environments and surroundings.

To the many families I have worked for:
Thank you for letting me come into your homes for the past many years to gain my experience and knowledge of cleaning.

To Vicki Lansky, my friend and publisher of my first two books;
Coming Clean and It's About Time. Thank you for having faith in me, and for making it possible for me to see places and do things I never dreamed of as a little girl in Missouri.

And most of all, to my mom:
You instilled in me an appreciation for cleanliness, organization, and love of God and family.

A note of caution
Care and caution are important when using the information in this book. Conditions and situations are unique to each of us. Products should always be tested in an inconspicuous area first. Always read and follow information on product labels. Common sense counts. Schar Ward disclaims any liability for the use or misuse of any product or idea presented in this book.

INTRODUCTION

In recent years, I've noticed an explosion in the number of self-help books people are collecting. I wonder, are they reading any of them, or does just owning the books make them feel better?

Everyone appears to be looking for better work habits, more self-esteem, ways to get organized, save time and help with their relationships. The increase of self-help books indicates to me one thing; parents aren't teaching children the life skills they need to cope with everyday situations.

Over time, I have watched parents become more and more busy. They drive for hours on a weekend to get their children to a sports activity that can last all day. They trudge through malls and large grocery stores to shop. They spend hours plugging into and updating their many electronic gadgets. All these things designed to improve their lives, have complicated them even more.

The need and desire for more time is rampant. So, what parent has the time and patience to train their children to clean? In earlier years, most of us lived in rural areas and everyone in the family had to help with the chores, children included. But gone are the days of doing chores like carrying in water, gathering eggs or hanging out laundry. Most kids today don't even know what a clothesline is.

Everything is done for us today. Automation has eliminated hundreds of jobs we once had to share with our children and the skills and principles that went with them. We need to step backward so our children can move forward. We need to go back to teaching kids to clean. It's so important they learn the satisfaction of doing a job and feeling good about it afterward.

Twenty years ago while doing in-home interviews for new cleaning clients, I would come across a closed bedroom door. When I asked if I needed to assess that room for cleaning, the answer was "No, that's my child's room and we don't go in there." The children are now grown, have homes of their own, and have no idea how to clean them because they haven't been taught that life skill.

It's my hope that this book will inspire you to teach children to clean, after all, the home is the best and first classroom.

Chapter One

START AT THE BEGINNING

Research about children cleaning

Research can be tedious, but did you even know research has been done on the subject of children and cleaning?

It appears that if you want your children to be responsible and self-reliant as they grow into young adults, it can be as simple as teaching them to set the table, pick up toys and help with the laundry! Who knew it was that easy? You just wanted some help around the house and now you find out that teaching your children to clean could be the most important thing you can do for them!

Marty Rossman, former associate professor of family education at the University of Minnesota, did a survey of children who had assumed an active role in 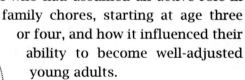 family chores, starting at age three or four, and how it influenced their ability to become well-adjusted young adults.

Rossman worked with unused data collected by Diana Baumrind, a well-known researcher on parenting styles. Baumrind conducted her study, using a sample of California families over a twenty-five-year period.

Rossman did a secondary analysis of the unused data collected by Baumrind and saw an enormous amount related to children's involvement in household tasks. Rossman analyzed eighty-four young adults based on their parents' style of interacting, and their participation in family tasks at three periods in their lives: ages three to four, nine to ten and fifteen to sixteen. She did brief phone interviews with them when they were in their mid-twenties. She used parenting styles, gender, types of household tasks, time spent on tasks, attitudes, and motivators associated with doing the tasks – to determine their impact on children. She measured each individual's successes and looked at the outcomes when they were in their mid – twenties. She focused on what they were doing in regards to completing their education or getting started on a career path, their relationships with family and friends, and whether or not they were using drugs. She also considered IQ's in her analysis.

Rossman was surprised with the results. One would think that IQ and motivation would have a strong bearing on success, but she found these don't matter as much as participating in household tasks. She analyzed it and re-analyzed it and still came to the same conclusion.

The study showed that when a parent waited to start their children on tasks at ages nine, ten, or fifteen to sixteen, the children thought the parent was asking them to do something they didn't want to do. They were far too self-centered and didn't understand the concept of working together as a family. Thus, the earlier parents train their children to take an active role in the household, the easier it will be to get them involved as teenagers.

Learning to clean may be even more critical than reading, writing or arithmetic, because if the only thing a child knows when he graduates from high school is "I am responsible for myself and my life," he will succeed.

If you allow and accept sloppy standards and poor

CHILDREN HAVE NEVER BEEN GOOD AT LISTENING TO THEIR ELDERS, BUT THEY HAVE NEVER FAILED TO IMITATE THEM.

James Baldwin

habits in your children at home, it will carry over into writing, speaking and other areas of their life. How they clean will be how they live.

Mark Simone head of the Navy Seals, says, "The first thing they teach a new Seal is to make his bed correctly and to make it the first thing in the morning. If the Seal has a bad day, at least they come home to a made bed and the knowledge they have done something right that day." Teaching yourself to do one thing right every day, leads to doing another thing right, and the list just keeps on growing.

I hope this research, convinces you start teaching your children to clean, and to make it a priority in your life. Now, let's get busy getting you some help around the house and making sure your child has a bright future.

Chapter Two

DON'T YELL — TEACH

Tactics

Threats – are the most common and least effective tactic parents can use to teach their children responsibility. No one likes to be ordered to do something.

Yelling – "Go clean your room" won't get the room cleaned. Children can't be asked to do something they haven't been trained to do. I have seen children's rooms I didn't want to clean and I am a professional housecleaner! The bed is pushed against the wall, making it almost impossible to make. Some beds are decorated with dust ruffles, creating difficulty when trying to change the sheets. Or worse yet, they have bunk beds, a housecleaner's worst nightmare!

Children need lots of baskets, bins and places to put their "stuff". Even if their closet is small, storage containers will help keep it organized. Trust me, if you only do these two things - make the bed accessible and give them lots of containers, you will find their room will stay cleaner.

Setting an example - is one of the best ways to get your children to help around the house. If you complain about housework and neglect your home, they will do the same. When you tell your children one thing and you do something else, you give them a double message. Children pay attention to what you do. One of the worst things parents can do is to criticize each other about housework. Parents should treat each other with respect, even if they have different standards regarding housekeeping.

The martyrdom mode - Besides "Go clean your room" I believe that "Nobody helps me around here" and "Why do I have to do everything" are the most often heard complaints in a family household. The truth of the matter is, if your children aren't helping you clean, it's your fault. You are not taking the time to teach them basic cleaning skills, which you will regret later on in life.

Excuses - Parents have many excuses for not teaching their children to clean:

- The children are too little. (If a child can pick up a remote, turn on a television and select a channel, they can learn to clean.)
- The children have too much homework. (You are busy also; they need to share)
- The children are too involved in sports. (Parents need to keep things in balance)
- I can do it faster. (Just think how fast cleaning could be done with everyone helping)
- I can do it better. (Standards are necessary, but you

might be surprised at how well they will do in a short time with supervision.)

One of the excuses I hear a frequently is, "I'm busy and I have to pick my battles." I hope that after reading the research on children and cleaning, you realize how important it is for your child's future and choose the cleaning, as one of your battles.

Don't criticize – this is the surest way to discourage anybody from wanting to help you. Telling them their work isn't satisfactory, especially in public no matter how you say it makes them feel like they don't measure up. On the other hand, don't tell them they have done a great job when they haven't, this just enforces bad habits.

Discuss it – When something isn't just right, discuss it and lead them through the redo. Children need to have the proper equipment and training. So, you must start by showing them exactly what you want done and how it should look when they are finished.

For example: When I taught my daughter how to make a bed, I showed her how to make the bed and what I expected it to look like when she was finished. I asked if there was anything she didn't understand and then left her alone to do it herself. I returned to the room after fifteen minutes and we assessed her work I didn't criticize -I just asked her if she thought the bed looked like it should and if not, how she could improve upon it. We discussed her suggestions; we took the bed apart, and I left her alone once again to make the corrections. It took three attempts, but when we were finished, she could make a bed like a pro, and she was very proud of her work. In fact, I caught her several times showing her friends how to make a bed. I could have accepted the bed the way she made it and praised her for trying, but the result would not have been the same. Knowing they can handle themselves without someone directing is very motivating. When you suggest a lesson, say to your child "I'd like to teach you this skill so you can take care of yourself when you're on your own."

Condescending tone – When teaching skills make sure your tone isn't condescending and always try to explain the benefits of doing something a certain way. Such as, separating the clothes before washing them to prevent colors from bleeding onto other clothes.

Show them – You need to show them how it's done and let them take it from there. You would be surprised at how much kids already know about cleaning. It's better to teach one thing at a time. A child's attention span is short, and you want them to learn to do things correctly.

A beginning and an end – Children need to see a beginning and an end to chores. This is also true of most husbands. If you tell your family that Saturday is going to be a spring cleaning day you might find yourself alone on Saturday morning. It's better to explain that you need their help on Saturday and everyone needs to spend three hours doing their part to help keep the family home clean. Assign designated chores to each family member.

Write the tasks on a sheet of paper to pass out on Saturday morning. Each person needs to understand what is expected of them. Make sure you have all the necessary equipment and supplies to complete the jobs; nothing is more frustrating than having to wait for someone to run to the store to pick up forgotten items.

Standards – As your children grow older you may find that your idea of a clean room is a little different than theirs. To resolve this issue, ask them to write a job description for their room. After they write their job description discuss how their ideas are different and why. It will help them understand the reason for your standards and you in return will learn more about how they feel about their room. Talking about ideas is a great way to compromise. You must believe that your children are capable and let them discover it themselves, a little bit at a time.

LOVING A CHILD DOESN'T MEAN GIVING IN TO ALL HIS WHIMS; TO LOVE HIM IS TO BRING OUT THE BEST IN HIM, TO TEACH HIM TO LOVE WHAT IS DIFFICULT.

Nadia Boulanger

Clean the community – Take your kids on community cleanup days. After they clean up a five-mile stretch of highway, they will think twice before throwing something out of the window of a car. This experience will carry over to their room, home, and yard.

Associated cleaning – Ask the question; "What do you want to be when you grow up?" If they say a nurse or doctor, explain how people in that profession must keep everything around them in a sanitary condition to prevent infection. Whatever the occupational choice, show how neatness and cleanliness connect with the job.

Reinforce – Never fail to point out messy or disorderly things. You can do this while driving, walking or just visiting a mall. It can be something as simple as an overflowing trash container. Let them know how disappointing it is to see and how sad it makes you feel for other people to see this.

Likewise, when you are in a beautiful, clean park or building, express your happiness at seeing how everything is kept up so well and how good that makes you feel. This will help them to connect cleanliness with good feelings.

Personal Cleanliness – Keep enforcing the idea that being neat and clean has personal benefits. Say things like;" Notice you feel better." "Your toys last longer when they are taken care of." "You can find things easier." Use every opportunity to stress the importance of cleanliness.

Praise – When a child does a good job of cleaning, compliment, compliment, compliment! But, only if it is a good job.

Reward – Giving rewards for cleaning, does work, if you do it right. The important thing is to think through the reward before you offer it and follow through afterward. Often, when we are in a hurry, we offer a reward just to get the job done and later we are unable to fulfill our promise. Breaking a promise is not a good example for a child. They lose trust in the parent and are less apt to help out next time it is needed.

Guilt – The last tactic is guilt. Never use this one. It goes like this. "You will be sorry someday when I'm dead and gone." Or "What if you didn't have a mother and father to tell you what to do?" Imagine how this must make a child feel? A child will sometimes use guilt to get something from you like "John's mom bought him a new bike why can't you get me one?" Don't fall into that trap, guilt shouldn't be used by parent or child.

Chapter Three

THE SECRETS OF HOW

Getting the Job Done

You've read all the reasons, and hopefully, I've convinced you that teaching your children to clean is the most important thing you can do for them. But, I can hear you saying "How am I going to accomplish this?" It's not as hard as you think. It will take a little patience, but the payoff is well worth it.

Real Tools

First, read through the **cleaning tools and supplies list** to make sure you have what you need to begin your teaching lessons. They need real tools to do a good job. When my granddaughter was four, my daughter gave her the cutest little toy vacuum cleaner. After playing with it for a few minutes she informed her mother that it didn't work, it wasn't picking up dirt. You can't fool the kids. They see these machines advertised on television and know what they can do.

Between the ages of three and six you should plug and unplug any electrical equipment such as vacuums into sockets for them, but after six they can handle that procedure also. Imagine their excitement to be able to use your cleaning tools!

You have real tools, you need real cleaning solutions, check out the **natural cleaning recipe** page. Children can have a lot of fun making these solutions. You will need to supervise, at least until they become familiar with making them. Provide them several kinds of essential oils to choose from; peppermint, tea tree, and wintergreen are excellent choices. When mixed and used correctly, these cleaning solutions are safe for your family and the environment. **Be sure to follow the directions regarding the masks when working with fine powders.** You can pretend you are concocting magic potions!

Make it Fun!

Inexpensive accessories can be fun. You can create badges for them to wear and pretend they work for a cleaning company. Give them a unique shirt or a cute little apron with their name on it. I have directions on the natural cleaning recipe page for making an apron out of a plastic garbage bag. Provide a small notepad, so they can leave you a pretend bill when they have finished cleaning.

When children are small, they love to help around the house. Cleaning at this time can be taught with fun and games. They love to mimic their parents, so watching you clean is a good experience for them and can also be an excellent bonding time. Too many times when parents want to clean the house, their first thought is to get the children out of the way so they can get it done quickly. The plan should be; what skill can I teach my child today.

As children mature, you will need to move from fun and games to work incentive programs. They will have realized that cleaning is work. But we will discuss that a little later on in the book.

You're Almost There!

You have your tools and cleaning supplies there is one more thing you need to do before you start cleaning. Make the area cleanable. You need to go into the room and look at it from a cleaner's point of view.

WE WORRY ABOUT WHAT A CHILD WILL BE TOMORROW, YET WE FORGET THAT HE IS SOMEONE TODAY.

Stacia Tausche

I have watched many parents spend a lot of time and money decorating their children's rooms and after it's all finished, the child moves in, makes the place a mess and the parents shut the door until the child goes off to college. If they had only put more thought into how cleanable it would be, they might have enjoyed the room a lot more.

So, the next step is to take the **room evaluation** chapter, go into your child's room and assess the room for cleaning. Circle each thing you need to change. Most of the things are so easy and inexpensive you can have it done in no time.

Chapter Four

NATURAL CLEANING PRODUCTS EXPLAINED

What these products are and what they do

 Some of these items you might have in your cupboard, but a few will require a trip to either the health food store or a supermarket.

Baking Soda

 Eliminates odors and works as a gentle scouring powder. It also has bacterial and stain removing abilities as shown in one dental care study, published in the Journal of Clinical Dentistry. So if it works on your teeth, it definitely will work on other surfaces too!

White Vinegar

 Vinegar's low pH and acetic acid content make it an effective cleaner for combating soap scum, alkaline mineral deposits, inhibiting mold and much more.

A 2010 scientific study showed that a 10% malt vinegar solution has been just as effective as commercial cleaning wipes in killing the Human Influenza A/H1N.

Liquid Castile Soap

An all-purpose cleaner, degreaser and disinfectant. Castile soap is made from vegetable oil. It's an excellent dishwashing liquid and can be mixed with many other ingredients to make safe cleaning solutions.

Pure essential Oils

An excellent way to enhance the natural cleansing properties of your cleaners. These potent, natural plant-based oils are environmentally friendly and biodegradable. Many of them have antiseptic, antifungal, antibacterial and antiviral properties and as a bonus essential oils, even provide some health benefits while you clean; for example, lavender calms the nervous system.

Murphy Oil Soap

This product is made with vegetable oil, and I have used it for years. You have most likely heard the argument about using this product on some wood floors. If you wash and dry your floors and use only the recommended amount of cleaner, you will have no problems. Any cleaning solution, will leave a residue if you don't dry it. When you dilute the soap in water, you can use this product to clean almost anything. It's easy on your hands and leaves a pleasant fragrance after cleaning.

Club Soda

A safe, effective window cleaner. It can also be used to treat difficult stains and spots such as chocolate, coffee and tea.

Borax

The common name for the natural mineral compound sodium borate. Do not confuse this product with boric acid there is a tremendous chemical difference between the two. The data sheet on borax gives it a safety rating of "1" which is the same as baking soda. I have been unable to find any studies that proved a danger to the Borax in natural cleaning products in diluted amounts as long as you don't get it into your eyes or ingest it.

Borax helps to eliminate odors, removes dirt and acts as an antifungal cleaner. Use with care around pets as it can be toxic if swallowed.

Natural Cleaning
PRODUCTS EXPLAINED

The Numbers

There are over 17,000 petrochemicals available for home use, only 30% have been tested for their effects on human health and the environment. Presently we know little about the implications of these products which we are breathing in often unknowingly on a regular basis. What we do know is that 5 billion pounds of chemicals are being used in the institutional cleaning industry each year. In addition to this, over 23 gallons of chemicals on average are used by cleaners alone each year and 25% of those gallons are hazardous.

The Smell

Cleaning products are everywhere, homes, offices, even in our cars! Did you ever stop to read what is in a car air freshener? They have that "delicious smell" because they are made with synthetic fragrances created by additional chemicals rather than natural scents.

We are spraying, burning and plugging in chemicals every day to get that "fresh smell" in our homes and vehicles with little regard to what it might be doing to our health.

Allergy sufferers often find their reactions are made worse by conventional cleaning chemicals used around the house. Many people have found that by switching to natural cleaners, their allergy symptoms improve dramatically.

The Cost

Natural cleaning solutions can save you money by reducing dependence on an expensive array of cleaning products. Most products sold in the stores are targeted to clean only one type of surface in your home so you end up with many different cleaning solutions.

Natural cleaning solutions can be used on multiple surfaces, saving you space and money.

Many of the key ingredients for making natural cleaning products are commonly found in your kitchen cupboard. Baking soda and vinegar are cheap to buy, and you can use them in cooking as well as cleaning. The initial cost of essential oils and Castile soap can seem a bit overwhelming, but they last a long time and are well worth the extra money spent.

We live in a throwaway world. We purchase disposable, diapers, cleaning wipes and paper products. If we can cut down on our use of some of these items, our environment will be a whole lot safer. For instance, by purchasing old 100% cotton and flannel sheets and old terry cloth towels from a Goodwill store, cutting them into pieces and using for cleaning cloths, we not only re-purpose an item but save a lot of money. The washable microfiber cloths are a good choice also, just stay away from disposable.

I must share this story with you since it aptly demonstrates what people have learned about buying cleaning products.

A Story

I was at a local Target store watching a young couple finish up their shopping. You could tell by the conversation that money was tight. They were having an argument about purchasing some disposable dusting wipes. The husband could not justify the cost, and she was screaming at him that

NATURAL CLEANING
PRODUCTS EXPLAINED

she could not dust the house without them! Really? This incident shows how dependent we have become on disposable products.

The Safety

Do you ever read the labels on the bottles of cleaners you purchase? Most people don't. If they do, they never get past the first 20 ingredients, none of which they can pronounce, and frustrated they give up and throw the bottle in the cart.

Most of the cleaners you buy at the store contain some pretty nasty stuff and my mom always said: "If you can't pronounce it, don't eat it or drink it." Sounds like good advice to me.

Natural cleaning solutions you make yourself are so much safer for you, your pets and your family.

Chapter Five

NATURAL CLEANING RECIPES

Making Your Own Safe Cleaning Solutions

Making your own cleaning solutions can be fun for you and your child, plus it's helping the environment. Most of the cleaners you buy at the store contain ingredients you can't even pronounce.

The cleaning recipes listed here are all made with safe, natural ingredients, but there are a few precautions you should take. I advise adult supervision when making these solutions.

- When mixing the fine powders such as Borax, be careful not to breathe in the powder. Keep your face away from the mixing container and wear a cold weather mask.
- Label your containers after mixing them so you will be able to identify them quickly.
- The cleaners smell good, so remind your child that they are not edible. They won't kill you, but you could become unpleasantly sick.
- Do not get the solutions in your eyes.

For children that are between the ages of five and ten, you can make your cleaning project, even more fun, by pretending you are magicians. Put on a cold weather mask, latex gloves, and an apron to make your magic potions! Add a pair of goggles for more drama. You can devise an apron for your child using a white plastic garbage bag. Take a small, large or medium trash bag, depending on the size of your little magician, and cut off the bottom. Slip the bag over their head using the drawstrings for straps. You might have to make a small slit in the hem where the string is encased to make it fit properly. Add a name tag identifying them as doctors of sanitation, dustography or sweepologist.

Supplies you will need:
- Medium size container, old mixing bowl or used ice cream bucket.
- Large spoon
- Funnel
- Cheese shaker
- Three plastic spray bottles
- Old catsup or mustard bottle
- Fork
- Labels and a waterproof marker

Nature's Soft Scrub
One and ¾ cup baking soda
½ cup water
½ cup Castile soap
A few drops of essential oil
Place all ingredients in a bowl and stir until mixture is the consistency of frosting. Add more water if it seems too stiff.

Store in an old catsup bottle. Shake well each time before using. This is a mild abrasive cleaner for sinks and bathtubs.

Carpet Freshener

Fill a cheese shaker ¾ full of baking soda

Add ten drops essential oil

Mix thoroughly with a fork Sprinkle on carpet before vacuuming for a refreshing smell.

All-Purpose Spray

Fill a spray bottle with half white vinegar and half water. Add ten drops of scented oil. If not scented enough, add more oil. Use to clean and disinfect almost anywhere. Spray on, wipe off and dry.

Window Cleaner

Pour one bottle club soda into a spray bottle. Kids love to spray window cleaner and club soda is so kid friendly and inexpensive.

Hard Water Build- up Cleaner

One teaspoon Borax

One tablespoon Castile soap

1/8 cup white vinegar

Two cups water

Five drops essential oil

Mix ingredients and store in a spray bottle

For removing lime deposits on tile and glass. Spray on the surface. Let sit for ten minutes, and rinse and dry.

Don't forget to label all your containers and store in a safe place. I hope you will find that making your own cleaning solutions is easy and fun. I can still remember helping my mom make her Lye soap which was the only cleaner we had when I was growing up. She washed our clothes, scrubbed our floors and cleaned our entire house with Lye soap. Imagine one cleaner for everything!

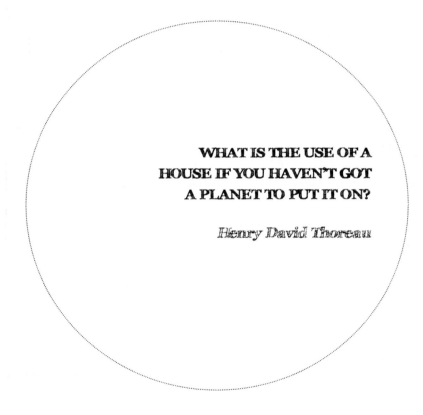

WHAT IS THE USE OF A HOUSE IF YOU HAVEN'T GOT A PLANET TO PUT IT ON?

Henry David Thoreau

NATURAL CLEANING SHOPPING LIST

Product	Where to Purchase
Baking Soda	Grocery Store
White Vinegar	Grocery Store
Club Soda	Grocery Store
Borax	Grocery Store
Liquid Castile Soap	Health Food Store
Pure Essential Oils	Health Food Store
Murphy Oil Soap	Target or Home Depot

The brand names of the products are not important. Any variety of white vinegar, baking soda or club soda will do the job. However, I do recommend Dr. Bronner's Castile soap, it seems to work the best. It also comes with a peppermint scent.

You can buy pre-packaged green cleaning products, but they will be more expensive.

 Unfortunately, the labeling requirements for green cleaning products are not well regulated. So, make sure you read the labels on the pre-packaged containers before purchasing them.

Chapter Six

CLEANING TOOLS FOR KIDS

Junior Cleaning kit

A child is just as capable of using most cleaning tools as an adult. Buckets need to be filled a little less full; squeegees can be ten-inch instead of sixteen inch and most cleaning cloths are "one size fits all."

Squeegee

A squeegee is used to remove water from tile and glass shower doors. Children will like learning to utilize this instrument. Teach everyone in your household to use this after they shower and you will never experience a hard water build-up on your tile. Squeegee's can be found at hardware stores and Target.

Pumice Stone

The pumice stone is used to get rid of the hard water deposits on **porcelain** sinks and lavatories. This tool looks like a rock, feels like a rock and when you are using the pumice stone on the porcelain it sounds like a rock. But don't worry, it will not scratch the porcelain. Just remember to keep it wet. Don't confuse this pumice with the one you use on your body; this one is specially designed for porcelain. You can buy the pumice at most hardware shops or big home supply stores, such as Home Depot in the cleaning department.

Bowl Swab

The bowl swab is a non-bristled, soft, absorbent cleaning tool. It looks like a large powder puff on a stick. It can be used to apply cleaning solution to toilets, sinks, and tile. When finished using, rinse it well and hang to dry. It's sold at janitorial stores and household supply stores.

Microfiber Wet Mop

I prefer cleaning floors on my hands and knees, but mops are fine if you have a good

one. Libman makes one that's lightweight, inexpensive, easy to use and is designed to get under and around furniture. Because microfiber attracts and holds dirt, rinse the mop well after each use and replace the mop head often. To prevent odors in the mop, pour baking soda over the head before rinsing it. You can purchase these at Target and Home Depot.

Brushes

You need three brushes, a tile brush, scrub brush, and a toothbrush. Buy inexpensive ones and replace them when they get too soiled or too ineffective to use. Use the tile brush to clean grout in showers, the scrub brush for floors and the toothbrush to get into hard to get to spots. Buy them at hardware stores or Target

Lamb's Wool Duster

Buy a long and short handled lamb's wool duster.

Short handle is used for a quick dusting of furniture and long handled for removing cobwebs from walls and high places. They're washable, and unlike feather dusters don't readily fall apart. You can wash the small duster in your washing machine. Put it in the washer with a terry cloth towel, a small amount of laundry soap and wash on a gentle cycle. After washing, remove it and let it air dry for a short time. It looks like wet dog hair when it comes out of the wash, but use your hairdryer to blow it dry and it will be nice and fluffy again. You can purchase these at a janitorial store or Bed Bath and Beyond.

Swifter Duster

If you like disposable dusters, this is a good choice. The handle extends so you can reach ceiling fans and high shelves, yet is short enough for tables and low places. The only negative is the expense of replacing the dusting pads. The dusters are available at most stores.

Bucket

A small bucket to hold your cleaning water. A used ice cream pail will work also. You can buy buckets almost anywhere.

The Caddy

A caddy to hold all your supplies as you move from room to room cleaning. You can find these at Target and Bed Bath and Beyond.

Cleaning Rags

100 % cotton for drying, terry cloth for scrubbing and soft flannel for dusting. The most inexpensive way to acquire these is at a Good Will Store. You can purchase old 100% cotton and flannel sheets along with old towels and then reduce them to the size you choose. It's always good to have lots of rags. The rags should be washed twice to remove all the chemicals. If you prefer microfiber – you will need one for dusting and one for window cleaning. The microfiber cloths should be washed by themselves as they attract dirt and the cloths will exchange dirt with each other. Microfiber cloths can be found Target, Home Depot and Bed Bath and Beyond.

Magic Eraser

The Magic Eraser is constructed of a sponge like material, it works well to clean refrigerator doors and walls. You can also use it to remove marks on walls and painted woodwork. Buy at Target.

Rag Bag
A place to store your cleaning cloths and handy to carry with you room to room while cleaning.

Rubber Gloves
Rubber gloves are essential for cleaning toilets or if you have sensitive skin. Buy almost anywhere.

Apron
An apron will protect clothes and make children feel like grownups. There are easy instructions for making an apron out of a plastic bag on my natural cleaning recipe page. You can obtain aprons at Home Depot and Bed Bath and Beyond.

Upright Vacuum Cleaner
A good upright vacuum cleaner is essential for cleaning carpet. I recommend buy-

ing this type of vacuum cleaner from a vacuum repair shop. The owners of these stores work with and fix them all the time and are very helpful in answering questions you might have. You can find them at many other stores.

Canister Vacuum Cleaner

A canister vacuum with attachments is ideal for vacuuming hardwood floors and upholstered furniture. I advise purchasing these at a vacuum repair shop also.

Broom and Dust Pan

These are good for a quick pick up of dirt and broken glass from floors. You can purchase these at hardware stores and Target.

Microfiber Mop

For use on hard surface floors, such as tile and wood. Several varieties can be found at Target.

Coat hanger

A coat hanger is one of the best organizing

tools, you can own. Simply hanging things up can make a room look a whole lot better. Buy at Target.

When possible buy pretty cleaning tools. Children are fond of bright colors. You will be surprised at how many cute cleaning tools are available, once you start looking for them.

Teaching children to clean up after themselves is easier if they have everything they need in one place. Give each kid a cleaning caddy with their name attached and filled with the basic cleaning supplies, such as window cleaner, paper towels, cleaning cloths and spot remover. When they have a spill whether it's due to cookie crumbs or soda pop, instruct them to get their cleaning kit, this book and get busy cleaning up. You will be amazed at how well they will respond when you make it simple for them. Pretty soon all you will have to say is "Ready-Set-Go! And they will take it from there!

SAFETY FIRST

How to safely use cleaning tools and supplies

- Use a broom and dustpan to pick up broken glass or anything sharp. Don't ever try to pick it up with your hands.
  Special rules apply to broken CFL bulbs. See the special section explaining how to handle this problem.
- Never place your hand into or under any electrical appliance that is in operation.
- Don't lift over your limit. Ask help in moving heavy items.
- Don't plug appliances into over-utilized receptacles. Too many plugs could cause a circuit to overload.
- Check electrical cords for worn or broken places before using them.
- Remember that water and electricity don't mix well. Dry your hands before plugging or un-plugging an electrical appliance.
- Unplug appliances by pulling on the plug – not the electrical cord.

> **CHILDREN ARE LIKE WET CEMENT. WHATEVER FALLS ON THEM MAKES AN IMPRESSION.**
>
> *Haim Ginott*

- Unplug small appliances such as toasters before cleaning.
- Use a step stool to reach high places. Make sure the step stool is secure before climbing on it. Never use a chair for this purpose.
- Don't wear blouses or shirts with large baggy sleeves while cleaning. These can get caught on items.
- Do open windows when using strong chemicals.
- Be careful what chemicals you mix. Never mix bleach and ammonia together.
- Wear tennis shoes to keep your feet from slipping.
- Place a cloth underneath your bucket of cleaning solution. A pinhole leak could create a disaster.
- Check the carpet for small objects before vacuuming to prevent damage to the vacuum.
- Always read and follow manufacturer's directions for cleaning products and disposal of containers

Chapter Seven

CLEANING CHECKLISTS

The Checklists

The following pages contain checklists to teach your child to clean. The checklists will preclude you from having to re-solve a bunch of questions such as:" What do I do with this?" and "There isn't any place for this." With these lists there is no excuse; everything is spelled out for them. These are step – by – step instructions for your child to follow. If your child is old enough to read, you can make sure they have everything they need to work with, give them the list and take a nap!

Run through the list of cleaning supplies and equipment they will require to complete the task before they begin. Explain, that when they are finished cleaning, they will be graded on how the room looks. Also, make it clear what they can expect for compensation if this is something you have agreed to.

Small children will sometimes clean because they think it's fun, but older children are motivated by money. They need money to buy stuff, music, games, skateboards, and other items teenagers think are utterly necessary. Sometimes these extra things aren't in the family budget and this gives them a chance to earn what they want. Teaching a child that if they work and do a good job, they will get rewarded, is a good thing.

When your child is finished cleaning the room you need to inspect it. Walk through the room together and grade the item and explain the reason for the grade. Excellent work might get an A, good job a B, and shoddy work gets nothing. You can specify an amount of payment for each tier, whatever meets your budget.

Use the skill score charts to keep track of the work and the money earned. You may copy the charts so you will have several on hand.

If you don't want to reward them with money, you could try things like an hour later curfew, a ride to the bus stop or any other special treatment. I found money worked the best for me. If they clean, extra things like windows, blinds or spot cleaned walls; you can add a little extra to the total payment. If they skip out on you, and you have to clean the room, charge them what they could have made and deduct it from their allowance. A child needs to learn that there are consequences for their actions. By practicing this, you are teaching them responsibility and how to

follow through with a task. This will be an invaluable lesson later on in life.

Make copies of this certificate to reward a job well done. After they have collected a certain amount, they can turn them in for a prize. There are numerous ways to award children for cleaning, finding the one that works for your child shouldn't be too hard.

Chapter Eight

BEDROOM EVALUATION

Make it Cleanable

Grab a pencil and paper for taking notes; It's time to take a hard look at your child's room and determine how easy it is to clean.

If your kid is very young, I suggest sitting on the floor to make this evaluation. It's amazing how big things look when you are a little child. Try to look at the room from the child's perspective and ask yourself the following questions.

Bed

- Is it filled with stuffed toys?
- Are there too many blankets and pillows? One nice warm blanket or comforter is all a child needs, and this makes putting the bed together so much easier for them.
- Is the bed far enough from the wall so the child can move around it easily?

- Do you have bunk beds? If you must have bunk beds due to lack of space, don't push them against the wall.
- Is the bed covering washable? Washable comforters are easier to manage than bedspreads
- Do the sheets fit the bed? Sheets that have shrunk are hard to stretch over a mattress. If you want your youngster to make their bed, you must make it easy for them. I gave my children color coded sheets, pillow cases, and towels; this helped them to find quickly the bedding in the linen closet. Color coding works for organizing kids.

Stuffed Animals

- Discourage relatives from giving stuffed animals to your child. These creatures seem to procreate in the dark. Store excess animals in a mesh bag hung from the ceiling or wall hooks. There's a hanging plastic chain with clasps especially designed for toys, hats, and so forth that can usually be found at Bed Bath and Beyond. Stuffed animals attract dirt and germs, just one more reason to have as few as possible.

Toys

- Are there big toy boxes filled with toys? Big toy boxes seem like a good idea because they hold so much, but I found them to be a problem. A child will always want the toy on the bottom of the box, so the toys on top end up on the floor. Baskets, small boxes or see-through containers on shelves are better and safer as storage option for toys. Stackable plastic bins work well and take up less space.

- Are there broken toys or toys with missing parts? Dispose of them and also any toy your child has outgrown. If he has too many toys, box them up and store them for a while out of sight. If he doesn't miss them, give away or throw out the box. Parents should purge the toys, not the child. A child only parts with his sibling's toys.

- If you have bins or storage containers are they labeled? Labeling your containers will help your child quickly find his favorite toy. If your kid can't read yet, attach a photo of the item to the container. Now you can teach children to put their things away because there is a designated place for them.

Clothes
- Are there clothes all over the floor, bed, and chairs? Could this be because there aren't enough hangers? Besides making sure you have enough hangers you should dispose of outdated, outgrown or unused items. Typically, a child has a few outfits they like to wear and wears them often. Don't fight it! The fewer clothes, kids have to choose from, the easier it is for them to coordinate an outfit and dress themselves without help.

Place out of season pieces on hangers in the back of

the closet. For the daily wear, install hooks and pegs on closet walls. Make sure the hooks are at a level that your child can reach easily.

- A place for dirty clothes? Instead of a clothes hamper, buy two mesh laundry bags, one colored and one white. Hang them on hooks and have the child place the dirty white clothes in the white bag and the dirty colored clothes in the colored bag. The mesh fabric has more ventilation than a hamper thus reducing odors, and the laundry is already sorted for you. If you aren't too fussy about your laundry, you can just tie the bags shut and throw the entire bag of laundry in the washer and dryer. When the laundry is dry, have the child take the bag to their room and put the laundry away. If the bags are not too full the laundry should be clean, a little wrinkled from the dryer maybe, but no worse than letting laundry set in the dryer for days before taking it out.

Shoes

- Are there ten pairs of shoes without mates lying on the floor? Children have tons of stinky shoes. Providing shoe racks on the back of the door or closet gives them a place to put them. Or a basket in the closet designated for shoes will work also. Once in a while sprinkle some baking soda in the basket to freshen them up.

Storage

- Are there plenty of reachable shelves, drawers and cabinets for the children to store their books, clothes and "good junk?"
- Do the drawers and doors of storage areas open easily? Anything that's difficult to open probably won't be used.
- Are there lots of collectibles-small dolls and trinkets? If possible, get a cabinet with see through doors such as Plexiglas. Real glass could easily get broken in a child's room. Another good investment is a bulletin board. Kids like to see their awards, school papers, and posters hung up so think about covering one entire wall with corkboard. Another idea is to apply "chalkboard" paint to one wall. Your child might turn that one wall into a work of art.

Under the Bed

- What's under the bed? Are you afraid to look? Under the bed is a great place for storing seldom used items. Shallow containers will slide under the bed with ease, and if the space is filled, the child can't hide half eaten apples and old pizza boxes under there. One of the pluses of having a bed with built- in drawers underneath is more storage and less mess. The other advantage of this type of bed is it can eliminate a dresser giving you a lot more space.

Beside the Bed

- Are there water marks on the night tables? Kids have no clue how to use a coaster, so to protect the wood and make cleaning easier, cover the tops with Plexiglas that is cut to fit. It' easier to get old gum and used suckers off the Plexiglas. Just remove the whole thing and wash it thoroughly. Make sure it's dry before replacing it.

Sports Equipment

- Are you tripping over hockey and soccer equipment? In my opinion, no bedroom is ever big enough to hold this kind of stuff. You need to designate an area in the garage, basement, unused room or closet for all these things. They are too much trouble to move and clean around, plus the room never looks organized with these things taking up valuable space. If you have no other place for the sports stuff, try decorating the room with them. Mount the balls, bats, and gloves on the wall. You will find the kids will put the equipment away more often if there is a special place for it. As for all the hockey gear? I still think the garage or basement is the best place for this stuff.

Flooring and Walls

- Are the walls washable? Walls need durable, washable paint or wallpaper.
- How about flooring? Is it easy to vacuum or mop? Carpeting helps soundproof a child's room, and pat-

terned carpet helps hide spills and stains. Installing expensive carpeting in a child's room isn't a good idea, the floor gets too much use. Vinyl and wood flooring makes cleaning up spills easier.

- Small throw rugs usually just get in the way and end up in a corner somewhere, kind of like throw pillows on a leather couch, they never stay in place. Throw rugs live up to their name; they are dangerous anywhere in a home.

Wastebaskets

- Are the wastebaskets large enough? Children need large washable wastebaskets. Forget the wicker and ornate designs. Stick with smooth and clean looking.
- Plastic Liners will help keep the baskets clean and make it easier to empty them.

Lighting

- Is there enough light? Do the curtains and blinds open easily to let in more light?
- Are there any free standing floor lamps? These are easily knocked over and can be dangerous. If you have lamps, the lampshades should be smooth and easy to dust.
- Is there lighting in the closet to make putting clothes away easier?
- Is there task lighting for reading purposes?
- Storing a flashlight near the child's bed makes them feel safer and is handy when you lose power.

- Keep a few cleaning supplies in your child's closet. A roll of paper towels, a bottle of window cleaner, a dustpan, and a small broom. If supplies are nearby, they are more apt to clean up a mess quickly.
- While you are sitting on the floor, look around and determine how easily your child could escape the room in case of fire. Every family, should know where to go and what to do in case of a fire. Being prepared could save your child's life.

Now that you have made the room cleanable, it should be much easier for your child to keep their room clean and organized.

PERHAPS PARENTS WOULD ENJOY
THEIR CHILDREN MORE
IF THEY STOPPED TO REALIZE
THAT THE FILM OF CHILDHOOD
CAN NEVER BE RUN THROUGH FOR
A SECOND SHOWING.

Evelyn Nowen

FINDING PROFESSIONAL HELP

Professional Cleaning Service

If you have evaluated your child's room and decided it's too big of a mess for them or anyone else to clean in its' current condition, you might need to bring in the big guns, a professional cleaning company. But before you do that, here are some tips on hiring a cleaning company.

Experience: Ask how long they have been in operation. If the company has been in the industry less than two years, you might want to call another business. The longevity of a cleaning company speaks volumes about the owners.

Referrals: Check with your friends and neighbors, if they are happy with a service, chances are, you will be as well.

References: Ask for several references and call them. This is worth the time and effort. Remember, you are inviting these people into your home.

Shop Around: A company that offers free in home quotes is usually the best choice. I wouldn't place a lot of faith in a bid made over the telephone. I have owned a professional cleaning company for many years and we would never send a crew out without checking out the home and making sure we can meet the client's needs.

Insurance: Make sure the company has liability insurance to cover any damage that may be done to your property and worker's compensation insurance to cover injury to the cleaners. Ask if they are paying the required withholding taxes such as Social Security and Medicare. If they aren't and they get caught, you could be held responsible for them.

Equipment: Be clear as to what cleaning supplies they will provide. You won't always get green cleaning unless you specifically ask.

Chapter Nine

CLEANING THE BEDROOM

Supplies you will need:
- Club soda spray
- Cleaning cloths- terry cloth, cotton, and flannel
- Microfiber cloth for dusting
- Garbage bag
- All-purpose spray
- A small basket for stray items
- Canister Vacuum with attachments
- Upright vacuum or microfiber mop, depending on floor covering

Ready – Set – Go!

Strategy

Work from left to right, and top to bottom. This method helps you not to miss anything during the cleaning process. If possible, open a window to let in fresh air and put on some music to keep you motivated. Pick up stray items and place in a basket. Put away your cell phone until you are done cleaning. Use this strategy in any room you clean.

Dirty Clothes – Everyday

Put the dirty clothes in a dirty clothes hamper. Not enough room in the hamper? Take the remaining dirty clothes to the laundry room.

Hang- up – Everyday

Hang up clean clothes that are lying on the floor, bed and furniture. Not enough room to hang everything? Put the excess in a pile on the floor of the closet. No room on the closet floor? Take them to the basement or an unused room, and vow to go through them with your parents, the first chance you have and get rid of items you have outgrown or don't wear anymore. Put away extra shoes, if they aren't on your feet, put them in the closet.

Trash – Weekly

Pick up trash daily and empty wastebaskets into a trash bag once a week. Don't forget the gum stuck in the basket.

Bed – Everyday

Straighten and make the bed. If you haven't mastered bed making yet, get into the bed and pull the sheets, blankets and outer covering up to your chin, then slide out the side of the covers and place the pillow neatly on the bed. Put all the stuffed animals and pillows back on the bed.

Sheets – Weekly

Remove the sheets and pillowcases. Place them in the laundry hamper. Get clean sheets and pillowcases from the linen closet and remake the bed. How to make a bed is explained in chapter twenty.

Stuff – Weekly

Put away books and projects. If the project has been out for six months, it's no longer a project but a lifelong pursuit. Get rid of it! Cut out sections from magazines you want to save, put them in a file, and discard the rest.

Dust – Weekly

Remove items from the desk, and dust the desktop with a Microfiber cloth. Dust the items you removed from the desk before returning to their proper place. Repeat this procedure with each piece of furniture in your room. If you find a sticky spot left from candy or soda pop, spray a piece of terry cloth with the all-purpose spray and rub gently until the spot disappears. Dry thoroughly after washing.

Mirror – Weekly

Clean the mirrors. Spray the club soda spray on the mirror and use a clean cotton cloth to dry. Look at it from different angles to make sure you have no streaks.

Wall Art – Weekly

Dust pictures and other hanging objects on the wall with a lamb's wool duster.

Floor – Weekly unless you have a spill, then do it immediately

Vacuum carpet with an upright vacuum cleaner. If you have wood or vinyl, vacuum with the canister vacuum and floor attachment. To wipe up any spilled liquids, prepare a small bucket of water with a tablespoon of Castile soap or Murphy soap dissolved in it. Dip a terry cloth rag in the water, wring it out and wipe the spots. Use a clean terry cloth rag to dry it thoroughly. If you use a mop, you still need to dry the floor. Clean not just the middle of the floor, but underneath chairs, small pieces of furniture and underneath the bed as far as you can reach. You might be surprised what you will find under there!! You could find what has been causing that strange odor in your room.

Smudge Watch – Weekly

Spray a piece of terry cloth with scented vinegar spray and clean the light switches, doorknobs, and remotes, to remove all the germs. Who knows, this might even prevent pimples!

Eye-Check

Professional cleaners do an eye check when done cleaning. Cleaners look around the room to make sure supplies have not been left, and the room looks as good as it should.

BEDROOM SKILL SCORE

Amount Earned_____

Skill	A	B	C	D	F
Clothes hung-up					
Dirty clothes picked-up					
Organiza-tion					
Bed making					
Dusting					
Floors					
Waste baskets					
Extras					

Chapter Ten

CLEANING THE BATHROOM

Supplies you will need:

- Baking soda
- Club soda spray
- Nature's soft scrub
- All-purpose spray
- Pumice stone
- Bowl swab
- Hard water build-up cleaner
- Several terry cloth and cotton rags
- One old terry cloth towel
- Trash bag
- Small basket for stray items
- Squeegee
- Large plastic drinking cup
- Rubber or latex gloves (if required)
- Broom and dust pan or canister vacuum

Fill a small bucket ½ full with warm water and dissolve two teaspoons Castile soap into it. Take the supplies into the bathroom and leave your cell phone in your bedroom until you are finished cleaning. Being distracted while cleaning will slow you down, and it makes you more prone to forget to clean something. Stay focused on your cleaning and you will get done faster.

Ready – Set – Go!

Pick up

Pick up the towels, fold them in three lengthwise sections and hang them on towel racks. Empty trash from wastebaskets into a garbage bag. If wastebaskets are washable, dip a terry cloth rag into your soap solution, squeeze it out and clean the basket. Use a cotton cloth to dry the basket.

Remove rugs by folding them in half to prevent dirt from falling onto the floor. The rugs should be vacuumed off or taken to an outside area and shook well. You will replace the rugs after the floor has been washed and dried.

Prep

Vacuum or sweep the floor. Vacuuming removes all the hair and makes cleaning the floor easier.

Shower

Place the old terry cloth towel on the floor outside the shower. You will use this to wipe your feet on as you exit the shower, this prevents you from slipping and falling. Remove the shampoo bottles and soap containers from the shower. You will replace these items when you are finished cleaning the shower.

Spray the glass shower door and the tile with the hard water build-up cleaner. Exit the shower. You are going to let this solution set for ten minutes while you do something else.

Toilet

Take your bowl swab and thrust it down the throat of the toilet to remove the water. It will take several thrusts to accomplish this. Removing the water prevents the cleaner from being diluted when you place it in the toilet. Sprinkle the inside of the toilet with ½ cup baking soda. Then spray scented vinegar solution over the baking soda. It will bubble and fizz but that's ok, that is an indication it's working. Leave this set in the toilet.

Sink

Move to the sink area and put away items that do not belong on the counter like hairdryers, brushes, etc.

Turn on the faucet to wet the inside of the sink. Shut off the water. Pour some nature's soft scrub into the sink and scrub the inside of the sink with a terry cloth rag. Turn water back on and rinse the sink thoroughly. Dry with a cotton rag.

Spray counter with all-purpose spray, wipe, then dry thoroughly. Spray faucets with club soda spray and polish dry. Check the lower part of the sink cabinet for toothpaste drips and spots. You can clean the spots with a damp cloth. Clean the items that need to go back on the counter and place them in the proper place.

If there is a soap dish, remove the soap and clean the dish before replacing the soap. It can be washed in the bucket of Castile soap solution and dried with a cotton rag.

Mirror
Spray the mirror with the club soda spray where it's dirty and dry with a cotton cloth. Look in the mirror from several different angles to make sure there are no streaks. Always do the mirror after you clean the sink to avoid getting water spots on your clean mirror.

Ok- back to the shower
Return to the shower and fill the plastic drinking cup with water. Pour the water over the tile and doors. Continue filling and pouring until the cleaner is rinsed thoroughly.

Remember to step on the towel outside the shower door each time you exit the shower. This keeps your shoes dry and prevents falling.

Squeegee the shower doors and tile. Use a cotton rag to remove any spots the squeegee missed

Clean the shower floor. Dip a terry cloth rag into the bucket of castile solution. Remove the rag: keeping it very wet, and wipe the floor back and forth until it looks clean. Dry the floor thoroughly with a terry cloth rag.

Replace the toiletries you removed from the shower. Containing all your shampoos, conditioners, etc. in a wire basket, speeds up shower cleaning. If your shower is installed over a tub- always clean the shower before the tub. Otherwise, you will get have to re-clean the tub.

Bathtub

Run water into the tub to wet the surface. Sprinkle with Nature's Soft Scrub. Use a terry cloth rag to scrub the tub clean. Run more water into the tub to rinse off the Nature's Soft Scrub and dry thoroughly. Your bare hand should come up clean when wiped across the bottom of the tub.

Back to the Toilet

Use the bowl swab to clean the inside of the toilet. Swish the baking soda and vinegar solution around in the bowl, with the swab, until it looks clean.

If there is a hard water build-up (this looks like a dark ring at the waterline) in the bowl of the toilet, you need to use the pumice stone to remove it. Wet the end of the stone and use it as an eraser to remove the ring. It will sound like it's scratching the porcelain, but don't worry; it's supposed to sound like that. Continue rubbing the stain until it disappears. Flush the toilet after cleaning. Wring out the bowl swab and place it in the cleaning caddy.

Use your all-purpose cleaner to wash the seat, lid and entire outside of the toilet. Wipe dry with a cotton cloth.

Floor

You are almost done. Clean the bathroom floor like the shower floor. Pay particular attention to the area around the base of the toilet, especially if there are small boys in the household. When the floor is completely dry, replace the rugs.

Eye – Check All Done!

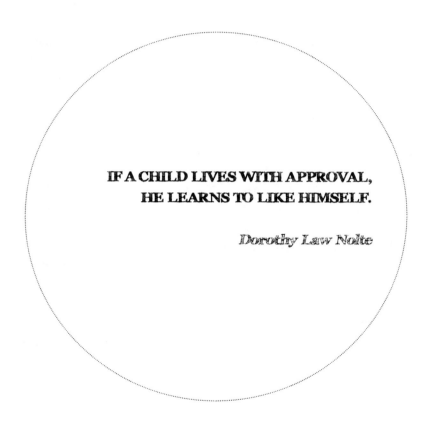

IF A CHILD LIVES WITH APPROVAL,
HE LEARNS TO LIKE HIMSELF.

Dorothy Law Nolte

BATHROOM SKILL SCORE

Amount Earned_____

Skill	A	B	C	D	F
Shower					
Tub					
Sink					
Counter					
Mirror					
Toilet					
Floor					
Extras					

Chapter Eleven

CLEANING THE KITCHEN

Supplies you will need:

- Nature's soft scrub
- Club soda spray
- All-purpose spray
- Several cleaning rags
- Castile soap
- A canister vacuum cleaner or broom and dustpan
- A bucket filled ½ full with warm water and two teaspoons Castile soap.
- Small basket for stray items.
- Mr. Clean Magic Eraser

Ready – Set – Go!

Countertops

Spray the all-purpose solution on the counters and wipe with a terry cloth rag. Dry the countertop thoroughly with a clean cotton rag. Make sure you move everything on the counters and clean underneath and behind each item. If you encounter a spot that has something stuck on it, cover the spot with clear water and come back to it after it has soaked for a while. As you move the counter items back into place, wash and dry each one. **Unplug all small appliances before cleaning them; such as toasters and coffee pots.**

Stove
There are several different kinds of stoves, but gas, electric and ceramic is the most common. **Make sure the stove is turned off and cool before attempting to clean.**

The top of the stove contains the heating elements or burners and drip pans. The drip pans get food spilled on them while cooking, so it's important to keep these clean. If the stove is gas, it's simply a matter of picking up the metal cover and lifting out the drip pan. Wash the pan with your castile soap solution, rinse, dry, and replace them

Most electric stoves require that you pull the elements in a particular direction before you can lift the pans out of the stove. This can be a little tricky unless a parent is there to help you. If no parent is available to assist you; lift the element and clean as well as you can with all-purpose spray and dry.

Ceramic has a flat surface so there are no parts to remove. In this instance apply some Nature's soft scrub with a wet terry cloth to any spots and rub them gently until spot is gone. Spray with all- purpose cleaner and dry.

This cleaning procedure works for all three types of stove:

Remove any debris such as pieces of food. Clean the top using nature's soft scrub and a piece of wet terry cloth. There may be spots where you will have to rub vigorously.

Rinse with your all- purpose spray and wipe dry with a cotton cloth. Clean around the knobs and check the front of the stove for any drips that need to be wiped off. If you removed the element, replace them. Rinsing and drying are the keys to making the stove shine.

Refrigerator

Since this is a general clean of the kitchen you only need to clean the outside of this appliance.

I see refrigerator doors that are covered with so many magnets and notes that it would take hours to remove everything. If this is the case in your home, clean as best you can. As you progress with your cleaning experience and decide you want to clean the inside of the refrigerator to surprise mom, chapter thirteen of this book has instructions for doing that task.

The handles and the water and ice dispenser on the door of the refrigerator get the dirtiest. Wipe these areas with all-purpose spray and a piece of terry cloth, then dry with a cotton cloth. If the refrigerator has a rough surface, use a Mr. Clean Magic Eraser instead of the terry cloth to remove embedded dirt.

Stainless steel refrigerators require extra care. Spray with the club soda solution and wipe with a cotton cloth. Dry carefully or it will have streaks. Leave the top of the refrigerator for a parent to clean unless you are a teenager and can safely climb a step stool. If you can use a step stool, wet the Magic Eraser and use it to clean the top of the refrigerator. There is no need to dry.

Microwave

Open the door of the microwave and remove the glass plate where you place the food to be cooked. Put the plate in the sink with water to soak. Use the all-purpose spray and a wet piece of terry cloth to clean the inside of the microwave. If there is food stuck to the inside surface, spray with all-purpose spray and let it set for a few minutes. **Any time you encounter something stuck to a surface, remember that soaking helps to remove it.** After cleaning, wipe dry with a cotton cloth.

Clean the outside with club soda spray and dry thoroughly. Wash the glass plate and return to the microwave.

Dishwasher

Only clean the outside of the dishwasher. Spray with club soda spray and dry thoroughly with a cotton cloth.

Floor

Always clean the floor last. Vacuum or sweep the floor to remove any loose dirt. If the floor is washable, use the bucket of Castile soap solution and wash and dry with terry cloth rags. See the instructions for scrubbing a floor in chapter fourteen of this book. You can use the microfiber mop if you prefer.

Eye Check All done!

**THE ONE THING CHILDREN WEAR
OUT FASTER THAN SHOES,
IS PARENTS.**

John J. Plomp

KITCHEN SKILL SCORE

Amount Earned_____

Skill	A	B	C	D	F
Counter Tops					
Stove					
Refrigerator					
Microwave					
Dishwasher					
Floor					
Sink					

Chapter Twelve

CLEANING THE FAMILY ROOM

Supplies you will need:

- Trash bag
- Cleaning rags-cotton, terry and flannel
- Microfiber dusting cloth
- Club soda spray
- Carpet Freshener
- All - purpose spray
- Small basket
- Lamb's wool duster
- Canister vacuum with attachments
- Upright Vacuum

Ready – Set – Go!

Pick up

Go through the room and pick up the trash and put it in a garbage bag. Take any items that don't belong in the room and place them in the basket to be put away later.

Upholstered Furniture

Connect the small brush attachment to the hose on the canister vacuum cleaner. Use the canister to vacuum upholstered furniture. If cushions are not attached to the sofa or chairs, remove them and vacuum the area underneath. You never know what you will find under the cushions, it could be enough change to buy a movie ticket! If you have pets, pay special attention to the furniture arms where the pets sometimes lay their heads.

Lamps

Dust lamp bases with a microfiber cloth. Don't forget to dust the lampshade. Some lampshades have small grooves in them. If this is the kind you have, you can vacuum them with the brush attachment on the canister vacuum. There is a place on the hose of the vacuum, near the brush attachment that slides open to lessen the hose pressure. Slide this open before vacuuming lampshade. Slide back when finished with the shade. **Be sure the bulb in the lamp is cool before cleaning.**

End Tables and Coffee Tables

Remove items from the tabletops before cleaning. Don't slide the items across the table, they could scratch the surface. If the table top is wood, clean with a microfiber cloth. If you find a sticky area, spray a piece of flannel cloth with the all-purpose spray and rub gently You want the rag to be just barely wet. Dry thoroughly with a cotton cloth. **Be sure the table is dry before replacing books or magazines.** If the tabletop is glass, clean it with the club soda spray. Spray on the cleaner and wipe until dry. After dusting the items, you removed from the table, return them to the proper place.

Bookshelves
The lamb's wool duster is very handy for dusting bookshelves and high places. A quick way to dust bookshelves is to take out two books on the top shelf, lay them aside, and dust the area where the two books were setting. Then move the other books on that shelf, into that space two at a time, dusting the area where they had been sitting. Continue doing this until the shelf is completely dusted, then replace the two books you had laid aside. Clean each shelf in this manner. Starting on the top shelf and working your way down, prevents any dust from settling on a shelf you just dusted.

Television
The newer television sets have delicate screens. All they require is a quick dusting with the lamb's wool duster.

Fireplace
If you have a fireplace, leave the inside cleaning of it to your parents. Vacuum the hearth with the canister vacuum cleaner. Remove any items from the fireplace mantel, dust the mantel with a microfiber cloth. Then dust and replace the items you removed.

Wall Pictures
Dust the pictures and picture frames that are on the wall with the lamb's wool duster.

Floor

If the floor is carpeted, sprinkle carpet freshener and vacuum with the upright vacuum. Start at one end of the room and vacuum your way to the door. Do small areas at a time moving the vacuum cleaner back and forth.

If the floors are wood, attach the floor attachment to the canister vacuum cleaner and vacuum the floor in the same manner as you would if you were using an upright vacuum. Wipe any spills with a terry cloth rag dampened with the all-purpose spray Dry the area well.

If the wood floor is very dirty, you will need to clean the entire floor with the hands and knees method of floor scrubbing or with a wet microfiber mop.

If the floor is only slightly dirty, you can get by using the microfiber dust mop.

The less water you use on a wood floor, the better. The important thing to remember is to always dry it well to remove any cleaner residue.

Light Switch Plates

Wipe the light switch plates with a cloth dampened with the all-purpose cleaner. Light switches get touched by a lot of hands, and hands have germs. Disinfecting them on a regular basis can prevent cold and flu viruses.

Door Knobs

Door knobs get used even more than light switches. Treat them the same as light switches.

Remote Controls

Very few people clean remote controls and just think of the things you do while holding a remote-eat, drink, chew your fingernails, scratch your body, and blow your nose. Now if that doesn't make you want to disinfect the remote, nothing will. Wipe with a cloth and some all-purpose cleaner.

Eye-Check

Take the items you placed in the basket earlier that did not belong in the living room and put them in their proper place. Do your eye-check and you are finished!

> YOU DON'T REALLY UNDERSTAND HUMAN NATURE UNLESS YOU KNOW WHY A CHILD ON A MERRY-GO-ROUND WILL WAVE AT HIS PARENT'S EVERY TIME AROUND-AND WHY HIS PARENT'S WILL ALWAYS WAVE BACK.
>
> William D. Tammeus

FAMILY ROOM SKILL SCORE

Amount Earned _____

Skill	A	B	C	D	F
Pick-up					
Upholstery					
Lamps					
Tables					
Book Shelves					
Television					
Fireplace					
Pictures					
Floor					
Extras					

Chapter Thirteen

CLEANING THE REFRIGERATOR

The refrigerator needs to be cleaned on the inside at least every six weeks. Keeping an open box of baking soda on a refrigerator shelf helps prevent odors.

Supplies you will need:

- Baking soda
- Cotton and terry cloth rags
- All- purpose spray
- Mr. Clean Magic Eraser
- Small brush
- Club soda spray
- A small bucket filled ½ full of warm water and two teaspoons of baking soda dissolved in it.

Ready – Set – Go!

Take-Out
You need to remove all the food from the refrigerator, one shelf at a time. Doing each shelf separately makes it easy to remember what was on each shelf

Wash

Wash the shelf with the all-purpose spray, dry with a cotton cloth. If you have any spots that are stuck or sticky, spray the all- purpose spray on them and let them soak for a few minutes, then wipe and dry.

Replace

Replace the food that was on the shelf. As you do this, wipe the outside of any bottles or cans. Follow the same steps for each shelf.

Drawers

The bottom drawers are called crisper drawers. You need to remove these and clean with a terry cloth rag dipped in the baking soda solution, then dry. Sometimes it's easier to do this in the kitchen sink. Use the baking soda solution to clean the bottom of the refrigerator before replacing the drawers. Remember to dry everything.

Inside Door

Do the inside door the same way you did the shelves. Remove the items, clean the shelf, and wipe and replace each item.

Rubber Part

A rubber strip surrounds the inside door of the refrigerator. This strip prevents the cold air from escaping the refrigerator. It collects moisture, so it's susceptible to mold. Clean the rubber strip with a small brush and all-purpose spray. Dry the area when finished.

Outside Door

The cleaning of the outside of the refrigerator depends on the finish. For a **stainless steel appliance;** use the club soda spray and dry the door it until it shines.

A **smooth enamel** surface door can be cleaned with the all-purpose spray or club soda spray. Just spray and wipe dry.

For a **rough surface** door, you will need to dampen a Mr. Clean Magic Eraser in the baking soda solution and wipe until clean.

A Rough surface door gets dirt embedded in the little pits, so it takes a little more rubbing to get it clean.

Grate

There is a grate on the bottom front of the refrigerator that requires cleaning The grate covers the area where the cooling fins are located. Keeping the fins dust-free will help the appliance last longer. This is a job better left to a parent; for now, just dust the grate with a damp cloth.

THERE'S NOTHING THAT CAN
HELP YOU UNDERSTAND
YOUR BELIEFS MORE THAN
TRYING TO EXPLAIN THEM TO
AN INQUISITIVE CHILD.

Frank A. Clark

Chapter Fourteen

LOADING A DISHWASHER

Dishwashers can be great time savers, but for them to do a good job, they need to be loaded properly. It's like any other household chore learn to do it in the correct way with the right stuff, and it becomes simple.

Ready – Set – Go!

Scraping

Prepare the dishes by scraping off the food. A rubber spatula will do a good job of removing food from plates and bowls.

Rinse or no Rinse?

There are two thoughts about rinsing the dishes before placing them in the dishwasher. Some say it's necessary and others claim that you don't have to bother that a dishwasher is supposed to wash dishes, so by rinsing you are defeating the purpose of having one.

However, if you have dried catsup or egg on a plate, do soak it off before placing it in the appliance. Rinsing isn't required, but ask a parent what their choice is-rinse or not.

Plates
Insert the plates into the wire slots in the bottom section of the dishwasher. They should face toward the center. Your objective is to keep all surfaces separated and accessible to the water from the sprayers.

Glasses, Cups, and Bowls
The glasses, cups, and bowls belong in the top section of the dishwasher. Stack them upside down so the washing solution can reach the inside of the items.

Plastic Containers
The heating element is located in the bottom of the dishwasher; so place plastic pieces in the top rack to prevent them from melting.

Silverware
Put silverware and other utensils in the utensil basket with the handles facing downward.

Pots and Pans
Pots and pans should be turned upside down on the bottom rack.

Some things are not designed to be washed in a dishwasher, such as sharp knives, crystal and fine china. Check with a parent before putting any of these items in the dishwasher.

Soap

Fill the soap container with dishwasher detergent to the designated level. Some dishwashers have a rinse agent feature. If you have hard water fill this container with white vinegar.

Last Minute Check

Make sure there is nothing lying in the bottom of the dishwasher that can prevent the spinning arms from moving freely. Sometimes when emptying the dishwasher, a fork or spoon can get accidently dropped into this area.

Run the Garbage Disposal

Run the garbage disposal before turning on the dishwasher. If the disposal and dishwasher drain into the same pipe, it's important to run the disposal for five seconds before starting; this clears the drain of food particles.

Running the hot water a few minutes before turning on the dishwasher helps to heat the water going up into the dishwasher.

Turn it on

Close the door, select the proper cycle and start the dishwasher. Most of the time the dishwasher will be run on a regular cycle. If you have lots of dirty pots and pans, you can use the pots and pans cycle.

Most dishwashers give you a choice of whether or not to use the heat setting to dry the dishes. I ordinarily choose the heat cycle, but not using it saves energy.

THE GREATEST GIFTS YOU CAN
GIVE YOUR CHILDREN ARE THE
ROOTS OF RESPONSIBILITY AND
THE WINGS OF INDEPENDENCE.

Denis Waitley

Chapter Fifteen

SCRUBBING THE FLOOR

Supplies you will need:

- Small bucket
- Castile or Murphy Soap
- Several terry cloth rags
- Scrub brush
- Gloves if you prefer)
- Knee pads (if you prefer)

Ready – Set – Go!

Prep

Vacuum or sweep the floor to remove any dirt before you begin to scrub. I have found vacuuming works the best.

Move Furniture

It isn't necessary to move the furniture out of the room for this method because you dry as you clean. You can move each piece of furniture as you encounter it and put it back right away.

Water

Fill a small bucket ¾ full of warm water. Add one table-spoon Castile soap. Stir the soap around in the water.

Where to Begin

Begin at the farthest corner from an entry doorway. You want to scrub your way out of the room.

Area

You will be cleaning the floor in two- foot square areas. This method assures you don't miss a spot and prevents any water from sitting on the floor for too long.

Scrub

Insert a terry cloth rag into the bucket of pre-pared water. Bring the rag out of the bucket fair-ly wet.

Apply the rag to the floor and use back and forth motions to clean the floor. If you have a particularly dirty spot, you can use the scrub brush to loosen the dirt.

Dip the rag back into the bucket of water, swish it around a few times and wring it out. Take the rag and wipe the area you just cleaned.

Dry

The secret to a beautiful floor is to make sure you dry it well. Take two pieces of terry cloth, put one in each hand and put your hands on the floor. Use one hand to wipe the floor completely dry. The other hand that's holding the terry cloth, is to prevent you from falling and hitting your chin on the wet floor. Don't laugh; I have done it many times. Drying the floor removes any soap residue which can eventually dull the finish of a floor. Continue this method across the entire room, working from left to right. Notice that as you are drying, the drying rag gets dirtier than the wash rag. Think of all the residue you would have left behind with a mop.

THE GREATEST AID TO ADULT EDUCATION IS CHILDREN.

Charlie T. Jones and Bob Phillip

Chapter Sixteen

CLEANING A BOOKSHELF

Having a lot of books is nice, but having a lot of books and being able to find the one you are looking for is even better. Follow these simple steps to a neat and tidy bookshelf.

Supplies you will need:

- A microfiber dusting cloth
- Two empty boxes

Ready – Set – Go!

Empty
Start by taking all the books out of the bookshelf. Removing this many books may seem like an overwhelming task, but you will be surprised at how quickly it will go after you get going.

Dust
Dust the entire bookcase with a microfiber dust cloth. Be sure to include the sides and top of the bookcase. The

microfiber cloth is better to use than a damp cloth because you don't have to wait for the bookcase to dry before replacing the books. Water can ruin books.

Give Away
Place all torn and damaged books into a box to be recycled and the books you no longer want into another box to be donated to charity. The remaining books you will sort and place back on the shelves.

Sort
You want to keep all the same size books together. Sort into four piles, tall, medium, small and very large, such as picture books.

Start with the taller books and place them standing up with the spine or tittle facing toward you onto the tallest shelf. Begin on the left side of the bookcase.

Keep putting taller books together until you are out of tall books.

Repeat
Move to another shelf and do the same thing with the medium and small size books.

Bottom
On the bottom shelf, put the very large books that are too tall to fit on a shelf. Lay them flat with the tittle facing outward. You can place several on top of each other.

If you have bookends they help to keep books upright.

Organizing the shelves like this makes for a clean, neat looking bookcase and you will be able to find whatever book you are looking for quickly.

PARENTS ARE THE BONES ON WHICH CHILDREN CUT THEIR TEETH.

Peter Ustinov

Chapter Seventeen

SPOT CLEANING A CARPET

Oops! You just spilled a whole can of soda on your mom's new carpet. Now, what do you do?

If you clean it up the correct way, she will never know it happened, but it's not good to keep things from mom, so after you get it cleaned up, you should tell her about your accident.

Supplies you will need:

- Several terry cloth rags
- Carpet spot cleaner
- A small bucket of water
- Some heavy books
- One plastic Zip Lock bag

Ready – Set – Go!

Soak it up

Place a piece of folded terry cloth rag over the spot and stomp on it with your foot. Continue stomping until the rag is saturated.

Replace the soiled rag with a clean piece of terry cloth, and repeat the procedure. Keep doing this until the spot is hardly visible. Do not rub the spot with the cloth; this will only spread the stain.

Rinse
Dip a piece of terry cloth in the bucket of water and wring it out. Blot the spot with the cloth.

Spot Cleaner
Spray the spot with the carpet spot cleaner. Folex makes an excellent spot cleaner that's environmentally friendly. You can buy Folex at Home Depot stores.

More Terry Cloth
Place two pieces of clean terry cloth over the spot.

Books
Put two or three heavy books on top of the terry cloth. Wrap the bottom book that will be touching the terry cloth in a Ziploc bag. The bag will prevent the book from being damaged. Let the books set on the terry cloth overnight.

The next morning, remove the books, and the spot will be gone. The sooner you clean up a spot, the easier it is to eliminate. If you let the spilled soda sit on the carpet until you get back from the movies- the job will be a whole lot harder.

Rinse out the terry cloth rags in the laundry tub and hang to dry.

Don't use any of your father's law books or the family bible for this cleaning job. Use old books that no one will care too much about if they happen to get damaged.

KIDS ARE ALWAYS THE ONLY FUTURE THE HUMAN RACE HAS.

William Saroyan

Chapter Eighteen

CLEANING UP A BROKEN CFL LIGHT BULB

 Wasn't it fun playing ball in the house until you hit the lamp and broke the light bulb? If you have the new CFL Light Bulbs you can't just sweep it up, you need to take some precautions. A broken CFL bulb will release a small amount of mercury into the air, so it's important to clean it up properly.

Supplies you will need:

Two pieces of stiff cardboard
- Rubber gloves
- Cold weather mask
- Glass jar or two sealable plastic bags
- Duct tape
- Disposable wipes or wet paper towel

If the breakage is on the carpet, you will need a canister vacuum cleaner.

Ready – Set – Go!

Step One
Open the windows. Turn off air-conditioning and heating units if you have them.

Step Two
Have everyone leave the room, even pets, then close the door to the room. Remain out of the room for at least fifteen minutes. Do not walk through the broken glass.

Prepare
Put on rubber gloves and cold weather mask and return to the area. You must not let the broken bulb touch your clothes. If the bottom of your shoes come in contact with the bulb, wipe them carefully with a wet paper towel and put the towel in with the rest of the disposable material. If the breakage occurred on a hard surface such as a wooden floor, use the following procedure.

Cardboard
Use the two pieces of cardboard to pick up the broken pieces and place them into a glass jar. If using plastic bags, put one bag inside the other, then put the bulb in the bag.

Duct Tape
Tear off about an 8-inch piece of Duct tape and fold it in half and use to pick up the small pieces of broken glass. Put this in the disposal bag or jar.

Disposable Wipes

Use the disposable wipes or damp paper towel to clean the area where the bulb broke. Put these in the disposal container along with everything else. Seal the jar or plastic bag tightly.

Vacuuming is not recommended for cleanup of a CFL bulb because it could spread the mercury, but If the breakage happened on the carpet, you may need to use a canister vacuum cleaner to vacuum out the glass embedded in the carpet. Make sure the windows are still open, and the forced air conditioning and heating units are turned off. Then follow the same procedure explained above using the cardboard, duct tape and disposable wipes.

Vacuum the area, remove the bag from the vacuum cleaner and place it in a sealed plastic bag for removal of a hazardous waste site. Wipe the vacuum with a damp towel and put a new bag in the vacuum. Put the used towel in the plastic bag with the used vacuum bag.

Check with your rubbish company. Some companies will let you put the bulbs in the trash, if they are bagged properly.

CLEANING UP A BROKEN
CFL LIGHT BULB

Chapter Nineteen

SETTING THE TABLE

Supplies you will need:

- Placemats
- Silverware
- Plates
- Glass or Cup
- Napkin

Ready – Set – Go!

Setting the table is quickly following letter writing as a lost art. With all the practices, classes and parents working late, few families, even attempt to gather around the table anymore.

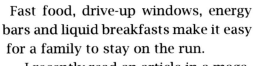

Fast food, drive-up windows, energy bars and liquid breakfasts make it easy for a family to stay on the run.

I recently read an article in a magazine, stating that colleges are offering classes on how to set a table. They have realized how important table setting is to society. Parents aren't teaching this skill at home and it's an everyday skill everyone should know.

Placemats

Making placemats is a fun thing to, especially on a rainy day. All you need is some thick paper, a marker, and silverware. If your children are old enough, they can trace the silverware onto the paper. Otherwise, you can do this task for them. You can color them, attach names, and decorate however you choose. If you want to be able to use them several times, you can buy some laminating paper from an office supply store and laminate them.

It's fun for kids to put placemats on a table. If you choose not to make them, you can purchase colorful mats at a store.

Plate

Put a plate in the center of the place mat.

Napkin

Fold the napkin in half lengthwise and place it to the left of the plate.

Fork

Place the fork on top of the napkin with the tines facing up.

Knife

Put the knife on the right of the plate, with the sharp edge facing the plate.

Spoon

The spoon is placed to the right of the knife.

Glass

Put the glass at the top of the place mat, near the tip of the knife.

A small vase of flowers (possibly ones picked by your child) completes the beautiful table.

A lovely table encourages people to sit, relax and enjoy good food. Some of the fondest memories of my childhood are when we gathered around the supper table and shared the events of the day.

Chapter Twenty

MAKING THE BED

It's important to make your bed, and it only takes about five minutes. In fact, it's so important that it's the first thing they teach a Navy Seal when they join the service. The Seals believe that doing one thing right every day, leads to doing other things right and this makes people feel better about themselves.

Supplies you will need:

- Fitted sheet
- Top sheet
- Pillowcases
- Blanket
- Comforter or bedspread

Ready – Set – Go!

Fitted Sheet

A fitted sheet has elastic around the edges; this helps the sheet stretch over the mattress. Check to make sure you have the right size sheet for your mattress. There are three sizes, twin, full and queen. There is also a king size, but it's usually not found in a child's bedroom. Unfold the sheet and lay it at the head of the bed. The sheet has pockets on each corner that fit over the corners of the mattress.

Pull the corner pocket of the sheet over the corner of the mattress nearest you. Pull the sheet to the foot of the bed and do the same thing with the other pocket. Go to the other side of the bed and repeat the process on those corners.

If the sheet doesn't fit properly, you might have the sheet turned the wrong way. Remove the sheet turn it around and try again. The sheet should fit snugly across the bed when you are finished. If you have someone to help, it will be easier.

Top Sheet

Spread the top sheet over the fitted sheet. The top sheet does not have elastic around it. You want the top sheet to match the bottom sheet in color, but it isn't absolutely necessary. The top sheet has a hemmed edge; this is the part you want to have at the head of the bed.

If the top edge has a design on it, make sure you place the sheet on the bed so the wrong side is facing down on the bed. This way, when the sheet is folded over the right side will be in view.

The hemmed edge of the sheet should stop at the head of the mattress, and the bottom of the sheet should hang over the foot of the bed. Try to make the sides of the sheet hang evenly on each side of the bed.

Start at the foot of the bed and tuck or push the top sheet in between the mattress and box spring until it looks neat. Repeat this procedure on the two sides of the mattress, pulling the sheet tight to remove any wrinkles.

Fold about four inches of the hemmed part of the sheet toward the foot of the bed for a professional look. Later on, you might want to learn how to make hospital corners and improve your bed making skills, but this is fine for now.

Blanket

If you want a blanket on your bed, you can put the blanket over the top sheet tucking it in between the mattress and box spring just like you did the top sheet. Or fold it and lay it at the foot of the bed until you need it.

Comforter or Bedspread

A comforter or bedspread can be spread evenly over the bed and straightened until there are no wrinkles. No need to tuck this in.

Pillowcases

Put the pillows into the pillowcases and place them neatly at the head of the bed.

Chapter Twenty - One

DOING THE LAUNDRY

Supplies you will need:

- Laundry Soap
- Color safe bleach
- Fabric softener
- Laundry basket

Ready – Set – Go!

Sorting

The first step in doing laundry is to separate the clothes. You will have three piles; whites, bright colors, and darks. There is a reason for sorting. If you wash the colored clothes with the whites, the colored clothes may bleed color and ruin the whites. You don't want your white socks turning pink.

Empty Pockets

Look in all the pockets to be sure nothing has been left in them. A piece of tissue or paper can create a terrible mess when it gets wet. If a piece of gum makes its way to the dryer, you have a real problem.

Check Stains

Examine the clothes for stains, such as grass or mud. If you find stains, pour a small amount of liquid soap on the spot and rub it into the fabric before putting the clothes in the washer.

Correct Temperature

Select the temperature for the wash. Most all clothes can be washed on a warm setting and rinsed in cold. Using warm water instead of hot saves energy. Check the tag on the clothes to make sure you have selected the proper setting on the washer. Certain clothes cannot be washed, and the tag will say dry clean only.

Load Level

Adjust the water level to the size of your load, small, medium or large.

Add Soap

Add the soap, following the manufacturer's directions on the soap container. If you have a fabric softener dispenser on the machine, add the softener now.

Time Wash

Put the clothes in the washer, but not too many. The clothes should lay loosely and fill about ¾ of the washing machine.

Too many clothes will prevent the machine from doing a good job. Three pair of jeans and four shirts is enough for one load. Close the lid, turn on the machine and let it do its work. It will take about 45 minutes to wash a load.

Dryer

After the washer has finished, remove the clothes and place them in the dryer. Some clothes may need to be put on hangers to dry, once again, check the labels for that information. Remove any lint from the lint filter. Add a fabric softener sheet to the dryer if you didn't add softener to the wash.

Don't leave the clothes in the washer when they are finished washing, they could develop mildew and smell bad.

Dryer Temperature

Choose the correct temperature for your laundry load. Select low for delicate items or medium for most fabrics. If you have a permanent press setting, you are always safe with that choice. Close the door of the dryer and turn it on. It will take about 45 minutes to dry an average load.

Done

When the clothes are completely dry, remove and fold or hang them in the proper place. Doing this right away prevents the clothes from becoming wrinkled.

IF THERE IS ANYTHING WE WISH
TO CHANGE IN A CHILD, WE SHOULD
FIRST EXAMINE IT AND SEE WHETHER
IT IS NOT SOMETHING THAT COULD
BETTER BE CHANGED IN OURSELVES.

Carl G. Jung

Chapter Twenty - Two

HAND WASHING DISHES

Supplies you will need:

- Dish liquid
- Sponge or dishcloth
- Scouring pad (optional)
- White vinegar
- Club soda spray
- Baking soda
- Rubber gloves if hands are sensitive
- Apron
- Dish drainer or dishtowels

Some music makes the job more fun. I find washing dishes and listening to music very therapeutic.

Ready-Set-Go!

Scraping

Scrape off any food that is on the dishes into the garbage disposal or trash can. If you leave food on the dishes, it will make your dishwater get dirty quicker.

Residue Rinse

Dishes that are heavily soiled need to be rinsed under running water in the kitchen sink before washing. If you have a pan or dish that has hardened food stuck on it, fill it with water and set aside to soak for ten minutes.

Prepare Water

Fill the sink ¾ full of very warm water. The warmer the water, the more grease cutting ability you have. If you have a double sided sink, fill the other side half full of warm water and add a tablespoon of white vinegar. Vinegar kills germs and helps to remove soap residue. If you have only one sink, you will need to run water over each piece to rinse it.

Add Dish Liquid

Add a drop or two of dish liquid to the water in the sink where you are washing the dishes. Two drops should be enough soap, if not you can always add more, better too little than too much.

Dish Drainer

Place the dish drainer on the counter on the side of the sink where you are going to rinse the dishes. The dish drainer has a tray that catches the water as it drains from the dishes. The drainer should be placed so that the tray drains into the sink.

If you don't have a dish drainer, you can use a couple of folded dishtowels to place the dishes on to absorb the water. You can buy special absorbent mats for this purpose also.

The drainer has special places for putting the dishes. The plates stand upright, and there is a small container for silverware. Put the silverware into the container with the handles facing down. **Be careful when handling large, sharp knives.** Don't put them into the utensil container; lay them on their side on the drainer.

Order

Use a dishcloth or sponge to wash the dishes in this order: Glasses – cups – plates – silverware – pots and pans. The pots and pans are usually the dirtiest. Wash the pans last, to keep the dishwater as clean as possible.

If you notice the water getting dirty. Drain it and start over again. Empty the water out of the dishes you had soaking. You can empty the water into the toilet, just make sure you flush it down. Now wash the soaking dishes. Soaking the dishes loosens the hardened food and makes them easier to clean.

Washing

Put one dish in the sink at a time. Wash each piece thoroughly. Cups and glasses require special attention. Wash the rim, handle and the inside and outside of each dish.

While washing the silverware look carefully at the tines of the forks, they tend to grab and hold food residue.

Pot and pans sometimes need to be scoured with a scouring pad to remove baked on food.

Checking

Rinse each dish, either by running clean water over them, or dipping them into the vinegar rinse water. Give the dishes one last look to make sure they are good and clean. There is nothing more frustrating than getting a fork out of the drawer and finding egg yolk on the tines. Then place them on the dish drainer to dry.

Clean up

Empty the water out of the sinks. Remove any food that's in the sink plug and place it into the trash or disposal. Turn on water and run the disposal. Pour a small amount of baking soda in the sink and scrub well with your dish cloth. Rinse the sink with water- spray with club soda and dry with a soft rag to a nice shine. The baking soda is a natural deodorizer and will keep the dish cloth smelling fresh. Hang up the towels and dishcloth.

You can save a lot of water and electricity by hand washing dishes. If the chore is shared, one person gathering and scraping, one washing, and another rinsing and stacking, it can be family time and the job goes quickly.

PLAY IS OFTEN TALKED
ABOUT AS IF IT WERE RELIEF
FROM SERIOUS LEARNING.
BUT FOR CHILDREN PLAY IS
SERIOUS LEARNING. PLAY
IS REALLY THE WORK OF
CHILDHOOD.

Fred Rogers

Chapter Twenty - Three

CLEANING UP AFTER PETS

You walk by the Pet Store and your child spies this cute little kitty, and immediately begins begging to have one. You look at the kitty and your heart says yes, but your head says no, and so the debate begins between you and your child.

But, before you give in, questions to ask yourself and your child:

Is your lifestyle conducive to owning a pet? Pets take time. You must exercise, train, love, groom and clean up after them.

Do you have the space needed for a pet?

They need space to live and move around.

Is there money in your budget for a pet? They require vaccinations, vet bills, licenses, food, and accessories.

Discuss these things with your child and make it clear that being a pet owner is a big responsibility. If they want a pet, they should agree to all the conditions that come with owning one. I can't help you with the decision to own a pet, but I can show your child how to do their pet clean up.

In this chapter, I tackled the three hardest clean up problems, gerbil cage, litter box and fish tank.

Chapter Twenty - Four

CLEANING A FISH TANK

Children are fascinated with fish. When children are small, they are usually happy with a fish bowl. But, as they grow older they want a tank with more fish, which means more work. A dirty fish tank not only looks bad, but smells bad.

Supplies you will need:

- Wet and dry vacuum cleaner
- An old nylon stocking
- Rubber bands
- Small brushes
- Disposable gloves
- Algae scrubber
- White vinegar
- Fishnet
- A clean cotton cloth
- Several clean terry cloth rags
- A new pail that you use only for tank cleaning- nothing else.
- Properly prepared water- to replace the water you re-

move from the tank. Prepared water is water treated with a water conditioner from the pet store and let sit until it becomes room temperature for the fish.

Ready – Set – Go!

Unplug
Unplug the tank. Water and electricity don't mix well! Always unplug any small appliance before cleaning.

Prepare the Vacuum
Check the inside of the wet and dry vacuum cleaner. If it's dirty, empty it and wipe out the inside with a damp cloth. Take the nylon stocking and stretch it over the suction hose of the vacuum. Secure the stocking with several rubber bands. The stocking prevents the hose on the vacuum cleaner from sucking up the rocks in the tank.

Remove the Fish
Take some of the water out of the tank and place it into the clean bucket. Using a fish net, remove the fish from the tank and place into the bucket of water. The water from the tank keeps the fish in their natural environment while you clean the tank.

Vacuum
Use the wet and dry vacuum to vacuum out the dirty water from the tank. Push the hose around the rocks to remove the debris. The nylon stocking will prevent the vacuum from

sucking up the rocks. Do not remove all the water; leave about 1/3 in the tank.

Decoration

If you have algae on your decorations, you can use the water in the wet and dry vacuum to clean them. First, disconnect the vacuum from the electrical outlet. Put on a pair of rubber gloves. Open the lid of the wet and dry vacuum. Dip the decorations in the tank and use a brush to remove the algae from the decorations.

Glass

If you have algae on the glass of the tank, use a handheld algae scrubber to scrub it off. Above the water line, you can use a terry cloth rag dipped in white vinegar to clean the glass. Use another terry cloth rag dipped in clean water to remove any vinegar residue, then polish with a clean cotton cloth.

Put it Back

Return the clean decorations to the tank. Replace the water with the prepared water you have ready and waiting. Leave the fish in the bucket for 24 hours, and then return them to the tank. Don't worry if the water looks cloudy. It will clear up in a few hours. Empty and wipe out the wet and dry vacuum.

THE BEAUTY OF "SPACING" CHILDREN
MANY YEARS APART LIES IN THE FACT
THAT PARENTS HAVE TIME TO LEARN
THE MISTAKES THAT WERE MADE WITH
THE OLDER ONES — WHICH PERMITS
THEM TO MAKE EXACTLY THE OPPOSITE
MISTAKES WITH THE YOUNGER ONES.

Sydney J. Harris

Chapter Twenty - Five

CLEANING A GERBIL CAGE

What could be more fun than holding a gerbil? But, no one wants to cuddle a smelly gerbil, so, it's best to clean their cage at least every two weeks. Cleaning the cage will help to keep your gerbil smelling good.

Supplies you will need:

- Laundry tub
- Several clean terry cloth rags
- Small and large plastic bag
- One teaspoon castile soap

Ready – Set – Go!

Take Out

Take the gerbil out of the cage and put him in a safe place. A place where you know, he can't escape. You can put him in the bathtub if you close the drain and make sure the tub is clean, dry and free of soap residue. If you have a running ball, that would be a good option also.

Save

Save a cupful of their old bedding in a small plastic bag and set it aside. You will need this later.

Toss

Put the remaining soiled bedding in a large plastic bag.

Clean

Take the cage to the laundry tub. Fill the tub with about three inches of warm water. Add one teaspoon of castile soap to the water. Put the cage in the water; and scrub with a terry cloth rag. After you have cleaned the cage, turn on the faucet and let the water run over the cage until you can't smell any soap. Soap is hazardous to your gerbil, so rinsing is critical. Dry the cage with a terry cloth rag until it's completely dry.

Refill

Place fresh bedding in the cage. Now, add the old bedding you have stored in the small plastic bag. The old bedding helps the gerbil re-adapt to the cage because the bedding retains some of the gerbil's scent.

Food and Water

Rinse out the food bowl and the water bottle and refill with fresh nourishment.

If you keep your gerbil in a cage rather than a small tank, the bedding can create a mess. Placing the cage on a large plastic boot tray keeps the mess contained.

WHEN YOU ARE A MOTHER, YOU ARE NEVER REALLY ALONE WITH YOUR THOUGHTS. A MOTHER ALWAYS HAS TO THINK TWICE, ONCE FOR HERSELF AND ONCE FOR HER CHILD.

Elizabeth Stone

Chapter Twenty - Six

CLEANING A LITTER BOX

Loving and playing with a cat is fun, cleaning the litter box; not so much. But, when you own a kitty someone has to do the job. If a child wants a pet, it should be their responsibility to take care of it. The child should be taught to feed, water, exercise and clean up after their pet.

Supplies you will need:

- Large trash basket
- Trash bag for used litter
- A clean liner for litter box
- Several terry cloth rags
- Castile soap
- A laundry tub
- Baking soda
- A cold weather mask
- Rubber gloves
- Vick's Vapor Rub (optional)

Ready – Set – Go!

Gear up

Put on the mask and gloves. Place a small dab of Vicks Vapor Rub inside the mask. The Vick's helps to mask the smell of the dirty litter.

Ready the Bag

Open the trash bag and put it in the large waste paper basket. The trash bag is where you will be putting the used litter.

Remove it

Remove the litter box liner from the box. To do this, grasp all four corners of the liner, and pull them together. When the liner is put together correctly, it should look like a bag of gold such as you see in cartoons.

Place the liner gently into the waste basket. There will be a lot of litter dust if you don't handle it properly. If the box doesn't have a liner, you will need to place the entire litter box in the prepared trash bag. Reach into the bag and remove the litter box, leaving the litter in the bag.

Clean up

Fill the laundry tub ¼ full of warm water. Add one tablespoon Castile soap to the water. Insert the litter box in the laundry tub and scrub with a piece of terry cloth rag.

After the box is cleaned, let the water out of the tub. Turn on the faucet and rinse the litter box in cool running water until there is no soap residue left in the box. Remove the box from the tub and dry thoroughly with a clean terry cloth rag. Rinse the tub with running water and dry with a piece of terry cloth rag.

Replace it

Put down old newspapers where the box will set. You can also use a plastic boot tray, such as the one used for boots in the winter. The boot tray helps to prevent the spread of the litter mix.

When the box is completely dry, place ½ cup of baking soda into the dry box. The baking soda is a natural deodorizer and will help to keep the litter box smelling fresh. Put a new liner in the box, and adjust it, so the liner will be easy to remove, the next time you need to clean the box. Replace the top of the box and latch if necessary.

Chapter Twenty - Seven

CLEANING GAMES CAN MAKE CLEANING FUN!

Instead of thinking of children as a cleaning problem, consider them as part of the solution!

You can turn cleaning into a game or adventure for young children. Most children love to vacuum with a small hand vacuum cleaner. Give them a dusting cloth and have them race you in the job of dusting to a finish point. Provide a cute little shopping cart to go from room to room, picking up their toys. Make the games no more than fifteen minutes, so you hold their interest, and they don't get bored.

Simon Says "Clean"

Tell the children "Simon is going to help us pick up all the toys and put them away."

Start by saying, "Simon says to pick up ten Lego's and put them in a bin." The child who puts away ten Lego's first gets to be Simon next. If the child says "Pick up ten Lego's" without prefacing it with Simon says, the child has to put the Lego's away himself.

Beat the Clock!

Set a kitchen timer for an allotted amount of time. Instruct your child to pick up the toys. If they complete the chore before the timer goes off, they receive a small reward. A reward could be an extra story or fifteen minutes of video game time.

A Clean Hunt

Place treasures in small plastic bags in your child's room. The treasures can be treats or small toys. Tell your child that you have hidden four treasures in their room and they must clean their room in to find them. When they find them, they must bring them to you, and when the room is clean, the treasures are theirs to keep.

A dime at a Time

Hide ten dimes in your child's room and tell them they must straighten their room to find them.

Musical Cleaning

Place a CD player in the area you want your child to clean. Allow your child to listen to the player while they work. Explain that they need to get the specified chore done by the time the six tracks play. Typically, each track is between three and four minutes long, so don't have too big of a task. If they complete the task in the allotted time they get a reward.

Giving coupons, that children can collect to turn in for favors or prizes. The more coupons the bigger the prize or favor.

Outer Space

Have your children pretend they are a spaceship, and they must pick up all the debris left in outer space. You could have a special box with space designs on it for that purpose.

Washing Hands

Here is a fun song to have your child sing as they wash their hands. The time it takes to sing the song should make hands squeaky clean. Sing to the tune of Row, Row, Row Your Boat, and repeat the song two times.

Wash, wash your hands
Play our handy game
Rub and scrub, scrub and rub
Dirt goes down the drain

Cinderella

You and your child can put scarves on your head, get a bucket of water with a small amount of white vinegar added to it, and pretend you are Cinderella's scrubbing the floor on your hands and knees.

CLEANING GAMES CAN
MAKE CLEANING FUN

Mating Sock Challenge

Put all the clean socks in a basket, set a timer for five minutes and tell your children to see how many pairs of socks they can match up before the timer goes off. You could have a small prize for the winner.

I Spy!

To get help clearing the table after a meal, play I spy. Choose a person to be the spy. The person who is the spy calls out an item on the table. The rest of the group must pick up the item that's been called as quickly as possible, and put it in the kitchen sink. The person spying the most items could have extra dessert.

Sock Dusting

Give your child a pair of white socks to put on their hands. Let them dust the furniture with the socks for five minutes to see how much dust they can pick up. The person with the most dust wins.

Downton Abby

Purchase an apron and a maid's cap or a bow tie and white gloves from a costume store. Have the children dress up and pretend they are living in a Castle and ask them to pick up the house. You can say things like "Oh my! Just look at this mess we have here!" Or "tut, tut look what the children have left lying about." You could share a spot of tea when you are finished.

YOUTH IS WHEN YOU BLAME ALL YOUR TROUBLES ON YOUR PARENTS; MATURITY IS WHEN YOU LEARN THAT EVERYTHING IS THE FAULT OF THE YOUNGER GENERATION.

Harold Coffin

STASH BOX CHALLENGE

Each child is furnished with their very own stash box which they keep in their room. The stash box can be a basket, or even a cardboard box. A clock with an alarm is set to go off each day at a specified time. When the alarm goes off the children are to bring their stash boxes to a designated area. Everyone then walks through the house and searches for items that are places they don't belong. As they find objects, they add them to that person's stash box. For example, if Mary left her shoes out, they go into her stash box. If Tom left his backpack on the floor, that goes in his box. After they have searched all the rooms, the children dump their boxes and tally up their scores. They get one point for each item. The parent adds their score to a scorecard kept on the refrigerator or bulletin board, and the boxes are put away.

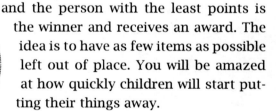

The points are totaled at the end of the week and the person with the least points is the winner and receives an award. The idea is to have as few items as possible left out of place. You will be amazed at how quickly children will start putting their things away.

STASH BOX CHALLENGE

This Week's Prize_____

This Week's Winner _____

Name	Mon	Tues	Wed	Thurs	Fri	Sat	Total

When We Clean Up Everybody's a Winner

Chapter Twenty - Eight

CHORE CHARTS FOR ALL AGES

This chapter contains chore charts for all different ages. Chore charts make it easy for a child to know what is expected of them each day. It gets them into a routine and children need structure in their lives.

You can use stickers and stars to mark the chart or you can simply use a pencil. Colored pencils make it more fun for the younger children.

The chores are organized according to what a child should be able to do at each age. Every child is different, so you may want to adjust the chores to what you feel your child is capable of doing.

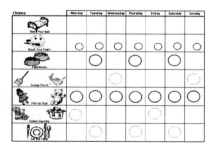

The age of three is a good age to begin teaching them to do small things for themselves. As they mature, you can add on additional chores as you choose. The important thing, is to help them understand, that every family member has to do their part in keeping your home neat and clean. Make them feel like a team, and always show your appreciation for the help they are giving you.

THE FAMILY FIRESIDE IS
THE BEST OF SCHOOLS.

Arnold H. Glasow

DAILY CHORES 3 – 5

	Mon	Tues	Wed	Thurs	Fri	Sat
Select clothing						
Get dressed						
Straighten bed						
Put dirty clothes in hamper						
Pick-up toys						
Put away books						
Feed pets						
Weekly Chore Empty Waste-baskets						

Download chart for printing at **www.uPublish.com/kidsclean**

DAILY CHORES 6 – 10

	Mon	Tues	Wed	Thurs	Fri	Sat
Select clothing						
Get dressed						
Make bed						
Dirty clothes in hamper						
Pick-up toys						
Clean-up spills						
Feed Pets						
Set table						
Clear table						
Pour cereal						
Bring in mail						
Take out garbage						

Download chart for printing at **www.uPublish.com/kidsclean**

DAILY CHORES 11 – 16

	Mon	Tues	Wed	Thurs	Fri	Sat
Get dressed on time						
Hang up clothes						
Put dirty clothes in the laundry						
Pick up books and clutter						
Make bed						
Set and clear table						
Help with meals						
Help with daily house pick-up						
Empty trash						
Feed pets						

Download chart for printing at **www.uPublish.com/kidsclean**

WEEKLY CHORES 11 - 16

	Week 1	Week 2	Week 3	Week 4	Week 5
Do your laundry					
Change sheets					
Vacuum or wash floor					
Dust bedroom furniture					
Take out re-cycling					
Clean a bathroom					
Wash the pet					
Plan and prepare one meal					
Help shop for groceries					
Carry in and put away groceries					

Download chart for printing at **www.uPublish.com/kidsclean**

MONTHLY CHORES 11 – 16

These are chores that help to eliminate a thorough fall or spring cleaning and earn extra money. It's a lot easier to do a few things at a time, than to try and accomplish everything in one day.

First Week	Second Week	Third Week	Fourth Week
Clean one bedroom window	Clean underneath Furniture	Remove spots from walls	Remove spots from woodwork
Clean baseboards	Clean blinds	Organize clothes	Dust lights
Dust Ceiling fan	Remove spots from carpet	Throw out old school projects	Wash wastebasket
Organize shoes	Clean on bedroom window	Organize drawers	Wash door handles
Wash any wooden flooring	Vacuum upholstered furniture	Vacuum carpet thoroughly	Dust walls with long handled duster.

Download chart for printing at www.uPublish.com/kidsclean

Each of these tasks takes fifteen minutes. Do one chore each day and your room will stay neat all of the time.

Chapter Twenty - Nine

OTHER LIFE SKILLS

In this book, I concentrated on cleaning skills, but there are several other life skills children should learn in order to manage their lives sucessfully. I have listed a few below for you.

Money skills
- How to Make a budget and stick to it.
- How to use an ATM.
- How to open and use a checking account.
- How to apply for a credit card and use it responsibly.
- How to open a savings account and set aside money.
- How to file and keep track of important papers.

Clothing Skills
- How to sew on a button.
- Iron clothes.
- Fold clothing properly.
- Pack a suitcase.

Emergency Home Skills
- How to locate and use the water shut off valves.
- How to locate and use the circuit breaker.

- How to use a fire extinguisher.
- How to perform basic first aid.

Kitchen Skills
- How to use a microwave.
- How to make coffee.
- How to operate the stove.
- How to handle a kitchen fire.

Automotive Skills
- How to pump gas.
- How to change a tire.
- How to check and add washer fluid.
How to check
    and add oil.
- How to check and add air to tires.
- How to jump start a car.

It's a parent's job to teach their children to become competent and self reliant. A simple mistake like putting too much oil in a car could end up costing them a lot of money.

Many years ago, it was quite common for people to get married at a young age and start a family. In fact, my mother and father was already married at the age of sixteen and lived in their own home. They had a garden, pigs, chickens and a cow, everything they needed to produce their own food. Mom canned food for the winter, made most of our clothes, and baked her own bread.

We were poor people, but as a child I never realized it, because I always had food, clothes, a home, and parents who loved me. They not only took care of me, but the neighbors if they needed help. Mom made quilts and rugs out of old clothes, crocheted booties for young women with new babies and they were both always ready to lend a helping hand where ever it was needed. They taught me how to live happily no matter what the circumstances.

A GOOD FATHER IS A LITTLE BIT OF A MOTHER.

Lee Salk

OTHER LIFE SKILLS

The Author

"By the time a child is sixteen, they should be able to clean every room in the house."

Schar Ward

Schar Ward credits her mother with instilling in her many years ago a passion for cleaning while living on a farm in Linn Missouri.

At the age of twenty-one, she married and moved with her husband to St. Paul, Minnesota, where she began a job as a professional housecleaner. Her meticulous cleaning soon put her in demand. In 1973 she started a small residential cleaning service. Within a short time, her service Domestic Engineering had grown to the point that she was employing several people and found herself with a corporation.

She realized the need for people to learn to clean properly and used her experience to write helpful cleaning books, she also began giving workshops that combined humor and hands-on cleaning help.

Book peddlers published Schar's book **Coming Clean Dirty Little Secrets from a Professional Housecleaner** in the spring of 2002. **It's About Time,** a book about time saving tips, was published in 2006.

Schar has appeared on HGTV, done television tours for Lysol, Murphy Oil Soap and Borax. She was the Green Cleaning Lady on the Twin Cities Live show in St. Paul, Minnesota for two years. Schar, also wrote a column for Dog Fancy magazine teaching natural cleaning for dogs. She has published numerous newspaper and magazine articles on cleaning.

Schar lives in Stillwater, Minnesota and keeps happily busy, teaching the world to clean.

CPSIA information can be obtained
at www.ICGtesting.com
Printed in the USA
FFOW03n2048130517
35445FF